Heaven's

Message

- How To Read It

Nowadays

Chris Stubbs

TRAFFORD
Publishing

Order this book online at www.trafford.com
or email orders@trafford.com

Most Trafford titles are also available at major online book retailers.

Printed in the United States of America.

ISBN: 978-1-4669-0675-4 (sc)
ISBN: 978-1-4669-0679-2 (e)

Trafford rev. 12/20/2011

 www.trafford.com

North America & International
toll-free: 1 888 232 4444 (USA & Canada)
phone: 250 383 6864 ♦ fax: 812 355 4082

Books written previously by the same author:

'Our Birth on Earth'

'When Scorpio Ruled the World'

To my mentors:

Dr. H. M. Duncan,

Head of Chemistry at Merchant Taylors' School for Boys, Crosby.

Dr. P. E. Eaton,

Professor of Organic Chemistry at the University of Chicago.

J. M. Addey,

Author of "Harmonics in Astrology" and

C. Harvey,

A True Inspirer of Astrology.

FORWARD

"The purpose of living is to discover the purpose of living."

Probably Astrology provides one of the keys to the solution of this puzzle by furnishing us with a method of self-judgement. Astrological principles represented by the planets may be related effectively to the study of human characteristics and behaviour, i.e. psychology.

However, this book is a practical one that describes basic natal Astrology for the 21st Century. Although we ourselves have hardly changed during the past seventy years there have been astounding scientific developments that have transformed our human situation. For example we have witnessed nuclear fission and fusion, the revelation of the structure of the common-to-all-life chemical compound, DNA, the enormous advances in television, communication and computing while not forgetting the tremendous developments in medicine and transport. All of these, together with significant increases in the understanding of life's deep-time origins, make God seem more remote, religion less relevant and atheism more acceptable.

But this book is not about science, not about computing and not about the abstract. It is a 'how to' book about producing and interpreting natal astrological charts, with illustrated examples, in order to be able to present completed horoscopes to potential clients. The budding astrologer should then be equipped to branch out into, and contribute to, the relatively under-developed knowledge of modern day Astrology.

"There is a book, who runs may read,
Which heavenly truth imparts,
And all the lore its scholars need:
Pure eyes and Christian hearts."

J. Keble (1792-1866), *'The Christian Year, Septuagesima'*.

Wirral, Merseyside, U.K., 2012.

CONTENTS

My thanks must go to Mr R. and Mrs S. Henwood and to Mrs J. Jackson for proofreading the whole book. Additionally they must go to my wife Angela for proofreading and in particular for 'polishing' the two Messages from Heaven presented in the book. Moreover, she and Mrs T. Beamer contributed valuable advice regarding the design of the book's front cover.

CHAPTER 1

A Genetic Understanding of Our Birth Process

"It is not so much the way you look, or what you are, although these are important,

But rather the way I feel, or how you make me feel, when I am with you."

The Earth-Moon binary system was created some 4.5 billion (thousand million) years ago probably by a large collision between the original (proto) Earth and a Mars sized body (Thea) having an orbit around the Sun similar to that of proto-Earth. Without the Moon and so without its role in generating birth processes, it is unlikely that life on Earth would ever have evolved as it has. We know that life has left traces of its existence here for almost four (3.8) billion years. Thus the Earth has spent relatively little time (only 700 million years!) as a lifeless planet following its binary creation with the Moon. The billions of years that have elapsed since the Earth first held life comprise the "deep-time" (compared with "deep-time", all of human time seems but a passing few moments) of joint biological evolution and geological change. We can visualise the Earth as a 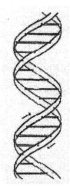 biosphere covered with a thin skin of tissue called life. Living things are composed of invisible, soft building blocks called cells, every one of which carries within itself a singular chemical called deoxyribonucleic acid (DNA). DNA consists of two long strands along which genetic material is bonded regularly. The strands run in opposite directions and are entwined like vines in the form of a double helix (see diagram). The genetic material holds the strands together tightly. Thus DNA is a large, life-chemical-compound made up from just five chemical elements, namely carbon, hydrogen, oxygen, nitrogen and phosphorus. DNA alone unites all life in a common history because every cell of every living thing has contained a version of DNA for a billion years. Because DNA can replicate itself, living things can produce offspring and so possess a common descent from shared ancestors. The breathtaking idea that a single DNA based life-form was the ancestor of all living things spawns a sort of "Big Birth" theory.

The growth of cells from a fertilised egg into a living creature is called development and the development of life on Earth is called evolution. Both development and evolution bring about structures of amazing complexity that are time-dependent and structured hierarchically, from the interaction of genes (entirely composed of DNA) with proteins. The DNA in every cell of a person – called that person's genome – is very like an encyclopaedia in design and content. We ourselves are very big compared to a cell, and cells are very big compared with the atoms of the chemical elements from which they, and so we, are made. We are composed of one hundred trillion (million, million) cells and each cell is made up of one hundred trillion atoms. Thus the complexity of a cell in atomic terms is about as great as the complexity of a person (brain included) in cellular terms.

Interestingly 99.6% of our working DNA is just the same as that of a chimpanzee. That residual 0.4% suddenly seems remarkably important!

Mutations

Mutations are the sudden appearance of a new, variant form, or behaviour (as in personality characteristics) that does not go away but rather breeds true in successive generations. These new forms, or patterns, are caused by changes in the sequence of bases (mainly four) in the DNA of a gene. The rigid, base-pairing rules, that enable information to be copied from one DNA double helix into two, can also fix in place any error that occurs. Even a single base-pair, if copied or repaired wrongly, just once, can completely change the meaning in all subsequent generations of that DNA.

Mutations are rare, but beneficial ones, since life is old, are the underlying cause of life's diversity. Without mutations life would have died out long ago from its failure to adapt to fluctuations in temperature, atmosphere and water level. With slight, but continuous mutation the descendants of some creatures have been able to survive myriad environmental disturbances to become the millions of different species that we recognise today.

Looking at this present richness of life on Earth it is difficult to believe that natural selection, that permits the survival of some, but not all, randomly occurring sequence differences in DNA, is responsible for so many different life forms. But every mutation can produce a new form, and each mutation must make sense in its own context, before it can serve as the new base line for the next mutation. In this way a series of changes will accumulate over time that will be seen with hindsight, but only with hindsight, as a remarkable parody of an intelligent plan. DNA's wasteful, but so far successful, strategy for surviving environmental stress and competition, through imperfect replication, drives Darwinian natural selection.

But for us, the rarity of general mutations means that, for all practical purposes, the DNA of the first, fertilised egg-cell, and that of all the cells of the resulting new-born baby, will be identical.

Biological Clocks

Studying Astrology gives us a feeling for time. All living things exist in both time and space. They function in time by using a variety of biological clocks, i.e. physiological processes that measure time using environmental cues such as the tides and light/dark cycles. These in turn derive from the Earth's moving relationship with the Moon, Sun and other members of the Solar System. Regarding Natal Astrology our attention is focussed on developmental clocks. Primarily these depend on our central nervous system (the brain, its stem and the spinal cord) and then on our hormone supplying endocrine glands, i.e. the pituitary and hypothalamus glands, that trigger the testes, ovaries and then the placenta to regulate pregnancy.

The Initial Stages of Our Birth Process.

Biologically, we can say that for every individual there are five steps that lead up to, and include, conception (see the Scheme). Within these five steps (say between steps 3 and 4) there is the mutual selection of the father and of the mother. The conscious result of the mother's DNA attracts the conscious result of the father's DNA, and vice-versa, in the process of sexual intercourse, or the selection of an appropriate mate. Love is important for the rearing of children because not only will you love those parts of the child that

SIMPLIFIED SCHEME FOR THE INITIAL STEPS OF OUR BIRTH PROCESS.

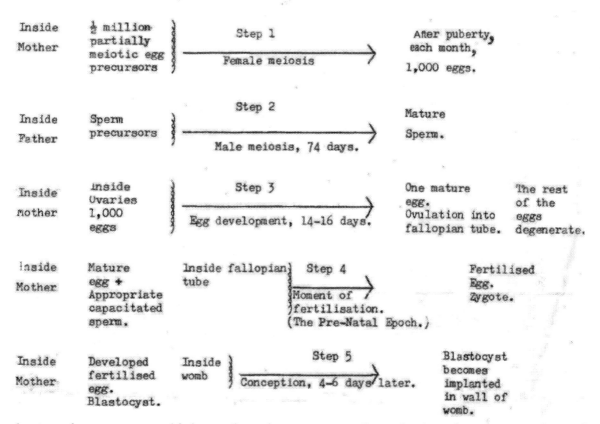

derive from yourself, but also those parts that derive from your loved one. The denial of this love selection process is perhaps one of the main reasons why most women find rape so abhorrent.

In steps 1 and 2, female and male meiosis leads to a multitude of eggs and sperm respectively, each different from one another, and yet each deriving from mother or father through multi-consecutive division by two. During step 3, roughly 1,000 eggs, out of an original half million or so, start development each month, from which only one, in general, becomes released from one ovary or the other. Similarly in step 4, only one, out of some 300 million sperm, plays the active part at the moment of fertilisation (astrologically called the epoch, i.e. the very beginning of somebody new). Even then there is a final screening in step 5 (conception), since not all fertilised eggs become attached to the wall of the womb.

Within these five steps the only obvious times necessitating planetary selection occur within the female meiosis (step 1) and within the egg development (step 3) stages, a fortnight or so before the epochal act of fertilisation (step 4). Hence the egg with the best gene fit for the characteristics of its time (given by the prevailing planetary configurations at the moments of epoch and of birth!) reaches maturity. Apparently nature, by necessity, is exceedingly wasteful of its genetic material in its efforts to produce one timely, new-born baby. Its approach for providing a timely birth is to swamp the situation with huge numbers. Thus the mature egg for the month has arrived by means of a two stage selection process from the mother's original egg-bank of half-a million. The father then supplies a vast number of sperm from which the pre-selected egg selects the first one with a correct gene-fit at the crucial time (step 4, the moment of fertilisation). At the moment of fertilisation (the epoch) not only is there a combination of the mother's genes with those of the father, but the sex of the baby-to-be is also determined. It is the father's invading sperm that carries the determining sex-chromosome. By the time of conception (step 5), when the wall of the womb either accepts or rejects a developing zygote (blastocyst), there appears to be no basic need for planetary influences; by this stage the genetic make-up of the potential individual is already well and truly complete.

Considerably predating the moment of fertilisation (step 4), and indeed the whole scheme, is the time when our own mother's eggs became established in her ovaries when she herself was but a ten week old foetus in our maternal grandmother's womb. Even at this foetal stage eggs begin meiosis that is halted before our mother's birth. Since any astrological significance here must account for all future offspring, some maybe decades hence, it is tempting to suggest that this can only involve the outer or "generation" planets. These foetal eggs then await their mother's adulthood, and further timely stimulation in order to develop into mature eggs that are then ready to initiate the next generation (us) at our moment of fertilisation (step 4).

Similarly, sperm that developed in our father's testes derived originally from primordial cells that migrated to his testes at an early embryonic stage in our own paternal grandmother's womb. Unlike eggs however, sperm are continually generated in vast numbers, each one reaching maturity after about 74 days ($\frac{1}{5}$th of a year). As they have no long, independent existence the meiotic process that produces them is relatively recent.

Thus we can see the links, <u>particularly down the female lines</u>, across three generations.

Once conception (step 5) has taken place, the development of the embryo, and then of the foetus, takes place rapidly, like clockwork. By the time that we are ready to be born (and the foetus itself appears to play a part in this) we are very much adult creatures in miniature.

- -

CHAPTER 2

Astrology, the Solar System and its Planets

'Keep it Simple', Joe Karbo, *The Lazy Man's Way to Riches*

The principles of the planets of the Solar System may be related effectively to the study of human psychology. This is no longer something fanciful but looks ever more real the more evidence we collect. For example, in the 1950s, Nelson found that the quality of radio reception on Earth varied with the angular relationships between the planets in the way that astrologers would have expected; Brown's team discovered that "biological clocks" were triggered mostly by the influences coming from the Sun and Moon, and the Gauquelins showed that certain planets, such as Mars and Saturn, in prominent positions with respect to the Earth (e.g. coming up over the Eastern horizon) occurred there significantly more often than by chance, for élite members of professional groups, such as athletes, scientists, politicians and authors. Thus the interested scholar can embark on a study of Astrology confident that, at the end, he will be able to produce interesting, credible and practically useful horoscopes for clients, without too much difficulty.

The Solar System

At school most of us will have come across the Solar System and the heavenly bodies of which it consists. The following list of its planets, placed in order of their closeness to the Sun, contains some facts about them that serve to remind us of our idea of what the Solar System is like.

Planet	Completes Orbit in	Inclination of Orbit to Zodiac	Period of Rotation on Axis	Mean Distance from Sun, m.miles.	Mean Velocity in Orbit mi./sec
Mercury	88 days	$7^0\ 0'$	88 days	36.0	30
Venus	225 days	$3^0\ 24'$	A few weeks	67.3	22
Earth	365 days	$0^0\ 0'$	24 hours	93.0	18½
Mars	687 days	$1^0\ 51'$	24½ hours	141.7	15
Jupiter	12 years	$1^0\ 18'$	10 hours	483.9	8
Saturn	29 years	$2^0\ 29'$	10 hours	887.1	6
Uranus	84 years	$0^0\ 46'$	10 hours	1784.0	4
Neptune	165 years	$1^0\ 46'$	15 hours	2795.5	3
Pluto	248 years	$17^0\ 9'$	?	3675.3	3
Moon	27.3 days	$5^0\ 9'$ (mean)	27.3 days	--	0.63

Notice, for example, that Pluto is almost forty times further away from the Sun on average than is the Earth.

The Solar System (see the foregoing, not-to-scale diagram) is shaped like a disc, or plate not a ball, consisting of planets revolving around the Sun (our star) at the centre, in roughly circular orbits. We can imagine a circular band around the edge of the plate, divided into twelve equal parts, that altogether constitute the circle of the Zodiac (the ecliptic) when seen from the Earth. The Earth has one satellite, our Moon, and it revolves around the Earth about once a month also within the plate of the Solar System. As the Earth travels around the Sun once a year it spins round once a day so that if we stood still for a day the whole circle of the Zodiac would appear to pass across the sky in front of us. However, the spin cycle, this time, is not aligned with the plate of the Solar System but is inclined at 23½ degrees (^{0}) to it. This daily circle, also divided into twelve parts, provides us with the Houses of Heaven.

"Planets" of the Earth

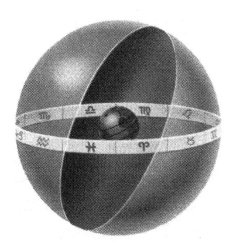

From the point of view of life, the Earth is our central station on which we receive the influences of the other planets (including the Sun and the Moon) as they circle around the Sun as we do in ever-changing mutual relationships. In other words, all the other constituents of the Solar System seem to behave as if they were the Earth's own planets. The diagram shows the Earth at the centre of the Zodiac (see the Table in the following chapter to identify the signs that the symbols stand for) but we could easily substitute an Earth-centred (i.e. geocentric) Solar System in its place (see the idealised, geocentric Solar System + Zodiac diagram that follows. This diagram is not-to-scale; the position of the Zodiac wheel is arbitrary and it is only shown for illustration purposes). Inspection of the diagram shows that, for this case, the Sun lies at the start of Taurus, the Moon lies in Leo and Mercury lies at the start of Gemini, etc. The ability to construct an accurate, geocentric map of the heavens for any time, date and place on Earth (⊕), which included the difficulties connected with the Earth's spin cycle, was a

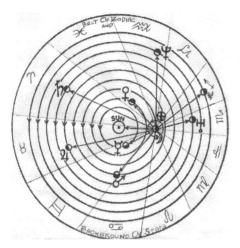

triumph of the Middle Ages. Now though, we let an astrological computer program carry out all the hard work for us. Traditionally, the Sun and Moon were called the luminaries, Venus and Jupiter were called the lesser and greater benefics and Mars and Saturn were called the lesser and greater malefics, respectively. Uranus and Pluto tend to be malefic, Chiron and perhaps Neptune tend to be benefic and the Sun, Moon and Mercury are the "neutrals". Those "planets" closer to the Earth (comprising the Sun, Moon, Mercury, Venus and Mars), and so those that appear to move more quickly around the Earth are considered to be the "Personal" planets whereas the slower moving outer planets, from Jupiter to Pluto and including Chiron, are considered to be the "Generation" planets. The belt of asteroids that lies between Mars and Jupiter will not be considered here in this introductory text but the major ones have also been considered previously by others.

<table>
<tr><th colspan="3">Personal Planets</th><th colspan="3">Generation Planets</th></tr>
<tr><th>Symbol</th><th>Name</th><th>Principle/Component</th><th>Symbol</th><th>Name</th><th>Principle/Component</th></tr>
<tr><td>☉</td><td>Sun</td><td>Will, Aim, Self-expression.</td><td>♃</td><td>Jupiter</td><td>Enthusiasm, Expansion, Generosity.</td></tr>
<tr><td>☽</td><td>Moon</td><td>Feeling, Response, Emotion</td><td>♄</td><td>Saturn</td><td>Sense of Lack, Fear, Cold, Limitation, Control.</td></tr>
</table>

17

☿	Mercury	Mentality, Communication	⚷	Chiron	Healing, Help, Philanthropy, Charity.
♀	Venus	Harmony, Affection, Relatedness	♅	Uranus	Independence, Sudden change.
♂	Mars	Initiative, Force, Energy, Desire.	♆	Neptune	Nebulousness, Fluidity, Impressionability
			♇	Pluto	Stimulation, Compulsion, Ease of discarding, Renewal.

We can consider that the principles of the planets, as a first approximation, represent the components of consciousness, as just shown in the Table. Notice that the astrological influence of the Earth (whatever that might be) is not listed because, presumably, it is the same for all of us. As the Earth is not really at the centre of the Solar System but orbits the Sun, then there are times when most of its planets appear to move backwards rather than directly, when seen from the Earth. This backwards motion is described as 'retrograde' and 'stationary' describes a planet's situation when it seems to change from direct to retrograde motion or vice-versa. When a planet appears to be retrograde its influence is diminished and/or modified but when it is stationary its influence is considered to be strengthened. Note that we never see the Sun moving backwards because it lies at the centre of the Solar System and we go around it. Analogously, we never see the Moon moving backwards either because it orbits the Earth.

- -

CHAPTER 3

The Twelve Signs of the Zodiac

The Earth orbits the Sun once a year. In this orbit we see the Sun from the Earth successively pass through each one of the twelve signs of the Zodiac. The Zodiac is a circular band of sky that extends about 8 degrees either side of the ecliptic (the apparent path of the Sun through the sky during one year). At all times and places on Earth half of the Zodiac lies above the Horizon and the remaining half below. Because we need a readily identifiable starting point, we decided long ago that the astrological year would begin at the Spring Equinox, i.e. when the Sun appears to cross the celestial equator (the Earth's equator projected out into space) and go above it when seen from the Northern Hemisphere. This occurs on or about the 21st March and the Sun then has left the sign Pisces and entered that of Aries*. We can detect the invisible Zodiac by noticing where the planets are at night .

The ancients recognised that nature/character/personality consisted of four elements, (not chemical elements) namely fire,

- -

*Each sign contains 30 degrees (written 30⁰), making 360⁰ (degrees) in all. Each degree can be divided into 60 minutes (written 60') and each minute into 60 seconds (written 60"). The symbols (' and ") are applicable to minutes and seconds of longitude; minutes and seconds of time are usually abbreviated as m. and s.

earth, air and water. Fire stands for ardent and keen; earth for practical and cautious; air for intellectual and communicative and water for emotional, unstable and sensitive. Additionally they recognised three ways of action (qualities) for expressing these elements, i.e. cardinal, fixed and mutable. Cardinal stands for outgoing; fixed for resistant to change and mutable for adaptable. These seven principles are cosmic/universal and abstract, whereas the Sun, Moon and planets are finite entities that comprise the Solar System. Although we have no reason to suppose that other star systems correspond to our own, there is equally no reason to suppose that the elements and qualities are merely local.

The twelvefold division of the Zodiac is constructed by combining the four elements with the three qualities. No one sign* is "better" or "worse" than another. Each one has its own strengths and weaknesses. Because human nature has remained essentially unchanged   since   ancient   times,   and   is   likely   to

- -

*Probably some of the names given to signs arose because people born when the Sun occupied one of the signs had a look of, or showed the characteristics of these animals. Perhaps others were named according to the type of weather and its consequences experienced during these periods. Possibly the constellations (groups of stars) were named after the signs with which they once coincided. Since ancient times, due to the phenomenon of the "Precession of the Equinoxes", these constellations now find themselves a whole sign out-of-place with the original Zodiac. The fixed stars that make up the constellations are not confined to the Zodiac; as we can see for ourselves they are scattered over the entire sky, but some do lie in the Zodiac, such as Antares, Aldebaran and Regulus.

remain so, then the derivation and properties of the signs are just as valid now, and for the future, as they were then.

For centuries we have arranged these twelve signs in their established order by considering their place in the zodiacal cycle of experience. For example, Aries (cardinal fire) initiates the cycle while Pisces (mutable water) rounds up the experiences of the whole cycle ready to begin a new one.

The principles of the planets manifest themselves in different ways depending on the sign of the Zodiac that contains them. Because each sign is of a different 'nature' the way in which each planet's principle works can be expressed by means of an appropriate adverb. Thus, we can interpret Mercury in Aries simply as "communication will be expressed assertively". Planets, whose principles work best in certain signs, or show their finest principles most effectively, rule these signs or become exalted in them, respectively. Conversely, when contained in signs opposite to these, they are considered to be in their detriment or fall, as their principles are not very compatible in these signs. A planet placed in a sign ruled by another planet is ruled by that planet and this is known as "disposition". The Table summarises the content of the foregoing presentation:

Name	Symbol	Meaning	Quality	Element	Manner	Ruler	Exaltation
Aries	♈	Ram	Cardinal	Fire	Assertively	Mars	Sun
Taurus	♉	Bull	Fixed	Earth	Possessively	Venus	Moon
Gemini	♊	Twins	Mutable	Air	Communica-tively	Mercury	Dragon's head
Cancer	♋	Crab	Cardinal	Water	Sensitively	Moon	Jupiter
Leo	♌	Lion	Fixed	Fire	Creatively	Sun	Neptune
Virgo	♍	Virgin	Mutable	Earth	Critically	Mercury	Mercury

Libra	♎	Scales	Cardinal	Air	Harmoniously	Venus	Saturn
Scorpio	♏	Scorpion	Fixed	Water	Passionately	Pluto	Uranus
Sagit-tarius	♐	Archer	Mutable	Fire	Widely, Deeply.	Jupiter	Dragon's tail
Capri-corn	♑	Goat	Cardinal	Earth	Prudently	Saturn	Mars
Aqua-rius	♒	Water-Carrier	Fixed	Air	Scientifically	Uranus	Chiron
Pisces	♓	Fishes	Mutable	Water	Appreciatively	Neptune	Venus

Notice also that the signs are alternatively positive and negative in that positive signs indicate expressive characteristics whereas negative signs indicate self-repressive or receptive ones. We see that all fire and air signs are positive and that all earth and water signs are negative.

Traditionally, the three mutable signs Gemini, Sagittarius and Pisces are called "double" signs because their versatility often gives them a dual nature. People having these Sun signs often have two careers, either at the same time or consecutively, and possibly two marriages. They also have more of a tendency to produce twins.

Because each sign contains 30^0 it is easily subdivided into three equal decanates of 10^0. The first decanate is considered to be more of the true nature of the sign while the second is influenced by the second sign in that element and the third by the remaining sign in that element. Thus the second decanate of Aries is influenced by Leo and the third by Sagittarius. In this case the decanate sub-rulers are the Sun for Leo and Jupiter for Sagittarius.

There now follows a personable yet distinctive summary of the characteristics associated with each of the signs, in order, as evidenced by persons having a strong emphasis of that sign in their horoscopes:

Aries, Cardinal-fire, Positive. Aries people are adventurous, pioneering, independent, relying on facts rather than feelings or theories, and have a happy, but vanity free, concentration on themselves. Success at work is important for them and they are likely to choose careers that combine plenty of energy with some, but not too much, theory.

Taurus, Fixed-earth, Negative. Taureans tend to be slow but sure, like to taste the good things of life and enjoy both work and leisure, taking pleasure in material possessions and affection. They shine in jobs concerned with money and the land which offer plenty of security.

Gemini, Mutable-air, Positive. Geminis tend to be fickle, unreliable and change their opinions constantly to suit themselves. They enjoy arguing and their conversation is full of twists and turns. They hate monotonous work needing jobs that give full scope to their agility and urge for change. They do well in work that involves mental change and variety such as publishing and craftsmanship.

Cancer, Cardinal-water, Negative. Cancerians are motherly, gentle people. Hard exteriors contain soft, vulnerable, easily hurt insides. Beneath their tough logicality they are moody and emotional. Their home-life is the keynote of their existence. They are good at jobs involving the home or children, or people with difficulties.

Leo, Fixed-fire, Positive. Leos are extrovert with a strong presence, vital magnetism and an urge to dominate. They do well in jobs that enable them to be in charge, or the centre of attention.

Virgo, Mutable-earth, Negative. Virgos combine intelligence with common sense. They are orderly, tidy hoarders and sometimes become obsessed with the need for cleanliness. They dislike unskilled work but relish replacing chaos with order, so that their neatness and desire for perfection gets full play.

Libra, Cardinal-air, Positive. Librans want to be liked and to like others. Their diplomatic natures make it easy for others to get along with them. Lazy physically, they do well in jobs connected with art, legal matters and dealing with others.

Scorpio, Fixed-water, Negative. Scorpios are reasonable, life-loving and honest but they can be difficult to get along with because of their secretiveness, fierce will-power and strong likes and dislikes. They like hard work and have a serious attitude towards life. Competitiveness combined with authoritarianism brings them success in military careers or in demanding occupations in which they can be tough and/or give orders.

Sagittarius, Mutable-fire, Positive. Sagittarians tend to be happy-go-lucky, often failing to take available chances. They are highly talented individuals with interests in almost everything. They excel at communication but can tackle anything that permits them some degree of freedom.

Capricorn, Cardinal-earth, Negative. Capricorns are introverted, submissive and self-effacing but extremely ambitious, burning to succeed. They go in for long, painstaking struggles that eventually take them to the top. They can excel at monotonous tasks that don't require much imagination, and where there are definite answers to most questions.

Aquarius, Fixed-air, Positive. Aquarians aim for personal freedom having little respect for convention or tradition if these obstruct anyone's liberty. Humanitarian, they take an intellectual approach, acting in groups for a social cause, for political reform or for environmental protection. They are open-minded, willing to listen but can be tactless and obstinate. They are best self-employed or occupied in work to help others.

    <u>Pisces, Mutable-water, Negative.</u> At best Pisceans are amiable idealists but can also be vague, devious and too liable to be influenced by others. They tend to oppose material values with spiritual ones. Lacking ambition and love of money they can work hard for a cause for serving others despite lacking dynamism.

- -

CHAPTER 4

The Twelve Houses of Heaven, Great Circles and the Morinus House System

Houses are different from Signs. They are stationary from the standpoint of the observer whereas all the Signs cross the Houses once a day, or so it seems. There is, therefore, no need to look for a suitable starting point for Houses. All we have to do is to arrange the twelve of them in the simplest, most sensible way for all natal charts. If we imagine ourselves at birth facing south towards the Equator from the Northern Hemisphere, then the centre of the 1st House (the Morin Point) lies directly to the left (to the east, the sunrise position), the centre of the 10th House lies directly over our heads, the centre of the 4th House lies directly beneath our feet and the centre of the 7th House lies opposite to the Morin Point and directly to our right (to the west). This arrangement provides us with the basis for the optimum, most symmetrical distribution of the twelve Houses around us.*

Every department of human life falls under one or other of the twelve Houses. The 1st, 4th, 7th and 10th Houses that correspond to the cardinal signs, are called 'angular'; the 2nd, 5th, 8th and 11th Houses, corresponding to the fixed signs, are called 'succedent'; and the 3rd, 6th, 9th and 12th Houses, corresponding to the mutable signs, are called 'cadent'. Angular stands for initiatory, succedent for resultant status and cadent for previously established situations and dispersed

- -

* Thus all rising planets will now be contained by the 1st House.

ideas/energies. Similarly the 1st, 5th and 9th Houses can be considered to be 'fiery'; the 2nd, 6th and 10th Houses as 'earthy'; the 3rd, 7th and 11th Houses as 'airy' and the 4th, 8th and 12th Houses as 'watery'. In a way similar to that used to describe the signs, we can present the general areas of experience of the twelve Houses, in order, as follows:

1st House: The person's personality, outward attitude and natural, easy, instinctive self-expression and self-centred interests.

2nd House: The person's belongings and resources whether physical, emotional, mental or spiritual, such as ambition to succeed and ability to acquire possessions.

3rd House: The person's relationships with his environment and mental attitude to everything to hand, such as relations and neighbours, as well as the means for effecting and developing such relationships/mental powers.

4th House: The person's home, parents, heredity, secure feelings, early life and retrospective retirement in old age.

5th House: The person's sexual life, courtship, and all activities from which the person derives particular pleasure or amusement. It covers innermost desires, children, pets, gambling and entertainment.

6th House: The person's health, food, clothing, craftsmanship and services either received or undertaken for others and for pets.

7th House: The person's partners, particularly the spouse but also business partners, i.e. those with whom the person seeks to combine owing to his/her sense of limitation; failure here produces those who openly oppose the person's aims in life.

8th House: The person's attitude to others' resources, such as wills, legacies and inheritance. It also stands for the person's ability to sustain relationships, to undergo regeneration and to survive losses.

9th House: The person's ideology, spiritual longing and the capacity to realise them through the increased perceptions, revelations and inspirations provided by religion, philosophy, science and prolonged travel.

10th House: The person's occupation, career and relations with superiors. It also stands for the person's attitude towards the community and the parent who guides the person's aspirations.

11th House: The person's hopes, wishes and friends, together with the mutual exchange of assistance. The person's social life and general attitude towards humanity also belong in this House.

12th House: The person's self-restraints, secret matters or associations, and external discipline/restrictions imposed by the army, for example, or even by being in prison. The person's complete integration with life thus belongs in this House.

The following Table summarises the foregoing presentation regarding Houses:

House Number	Description	Experience
1st	Angular	The Person, Personality
2nd	Succedent	Resource, Money, Feelings, Possessions.
3rd	Cadent	Brethren, Communications, Neighbours.
4th	Angular	Home, House, End of Life, Parent at home.
5th	Succedent	Pleasures, Love, Children, Self-expression.
6th	Cadent	Service in work. Health.
7th	Angular	Partnerships, Competitors, Opportunity.
8th	Succedent	Legacies, Regeneration, Life-force, Death.
9th	Cadent	Understanding, Religion, Profound interests.
10th	Angular	Public standing, Profession, Working parent.

| 11th | Succedent | Friends, Hopes, Objectives |
| 12th | Cadent | Retirement, Escape, Sacrifice, The Subconscious. |

The problem we have in constructing a suitable House system for use is trying to reconcile the fact that the Earth's Equator (the plane of its spin) is inclined at $23\frac{1}{2}^0$ to the plane of the Zodiac. We have the time, i.e. the time and date of birth, now all that we need is to create the correct space, i.e. the relationship of the Solar System with respect to the place of birth on Earth. Let's begin with the Earth itself and consider how best we can define its position within the Solar System.

Great Circles

Inside a planetarium, imagining that we are seated at the Earth's centre, we can look up at the domed ceiling of stars above us, and at the same time, imagine the continuation to another dome of stars beneath us. This whole sky of stars that surrounds us is called the Celestial Sphere. The plane of any circle that contains the centre of the Earth at its centre is called a Great circle. For example the Equator is a Great circle and corresponds to latitude 0^0. However, all other circles of latitude, parallel to the Equator, but whose plane cannot contain the Earth's centre, are small circles. On the other hand, if we think about it for a moment, all circles of longitude are indeed Great circles.

Diagram 1 shows the major Great circles of the Celestial Sphere. Probably the Meridian is the most important Great circle. It

Diagram 1: The Celestial Sphere (described for Polar Elevation of 53⁰ 25'N, the Latitude for Liverpool.)

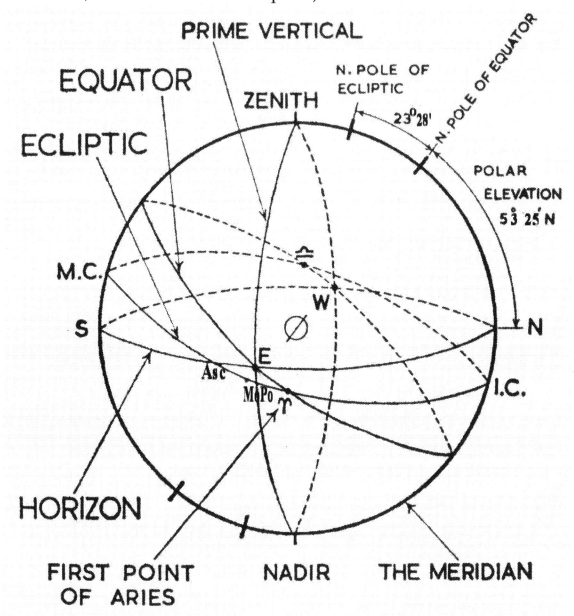

is the North – South Great circle and it passes through the North and South poles of the Equator, the North and South poles of the Ecliptic, the North and South points of the true Horizon, as well as the Zenith and Nadir (the poles of the true Horizon). The Sun crosses the Meridian at midday (anywhere on Earth) and this point of

30

intersection with the Ecliptic (the Sun's apparent path and the circle of the Zodiac) is known as the Midheaven. We can speak of three other Great circles: the Prime Vertical, the Equator and the true Horizon as secondaries to the Meridian because they all pass through the East – West points, the poles of the Meridian. The true Horizon must not be confused with the visible horizon, formed by the apparent meeting of the Earth with the sky, which is a small circle that is parallel to the true Horizon.

The Morinus House System.

Keeping our introduction of Great circles in mind we can construct our own personal map of the Zodiac, containing the heavenly bodies of the Solar System including the Sun and Moon. This is a picture/chart of the heavens as they appeared at the time and place of our birth on Earth. Nowadays we can do this easily using a computer and the appropriate software. Briefly, the first step in making/casting/erecting the chart is to calculate our star (sidereal) time of birth, unlike clock time, that is determined by the Sun. Anyone can do this by means of a very simple formula:

$$S + T + A + R = \text{L.S.T. of birth.}$$

where S stands for the sidereal (star) time at midnight (from an ephemeris -- regular data files of the positions of the Sun, Moon and planets) at the start of the day of birth; T stands for the clock (sun) time (corrected for summer time, if necessary); A is the correction factor required to convert T into star time (i.e. 9.86 secs. per hour) and R stands for "rectification" – the adjustment of the Zone time because the place of birth lies East or West of the exact longitude degree for which the Zone time is completely accurate. L.S.T. stands for the calculated local sidereal time that we require to find the Morin Point (the centre of the 1st House) from "Tables of Morinus Houses".

The second step is to calculate the twelve "Houses of Heaven" (also from the Tables of Morinus Houses). Now signs come from the yearly cycle and the Houses from the daily cycle. By superimposing these two cycles on top of one another, with the Earth at the common centre, we construct a chart of the heavens for each of our birth times.

Thirdly, we use an ephemeris to put the planets in the Zodiac, and finally list the various aspects (angles) they subtend at the Earth's centre (but thankfully the computer program carries out all of the contents of the last three paragraphs for us).

Note, however, that there are in fact several different ways of combining the twelve-fold division (the signs) of the Zodiac with the Houses. These methods all have their supporters and detractors but the method that we shall use was devised by the great French astrologer and mathematician, Morin de Villefranche, known as Morinus. His astrological logic proceeded as follows:

Our Earth itself is defined by the Equator with its axis passing through the North and South poles. At our moment of birth we can fix the position of our Houses by seeing where 1) the Meridian and 2) the true Horizon intersect the Equator. We now trisect the resulting quadrant formed so that, when all four quadrants have been trisected, we then have twelve equidistant points around the Equator. We take these points as centres (rather than the boundaries) of the Houses, thus making them more symmetrical about the place of birth.

To specify House centres in terms of the heavens we now have to apply the sky to the Earth. We define the sky by the Ecliptic (the Zodiac), the yearly apparent path of the Sun around the Earth, with its axis passing through its own North and South poles. The points where six Great circles intersect the ecliptic, each passing through the North and South poles of the Ecliptic, and through two different and opposite House centre points on the Equator, describe the House centres in terms of degrees of the Zodiac (see diagram 2). In other words House centres on the Equator are determined as "celestial longitude". Essentially, this is the House system proposed by Morinus. The first House centre, called the Morin Point, is the East point (i.e. the point of intersection of the true Horizon with the Equator) projected onto the Ecliptic. In a sense it is a triple E point, where the East point of the Horizon on the Equator is defined by the Ecliptic. The Morin Point is at right angles (orthogonal) to the Midheaven. Notice that the simple Morinus House System uses only Great circles in its construction. Thus it is independent of latitude and so is valid worldwide. This suggests that our birth on Earth is more of the Earth (i.e. just longitude) than it is of the birthplace on Earth (i.e. both longitude and latitude). Additionally, the Houses it creates are all roughly the same size (as required from first principles, which dispenses with signs of long and short Ascension) and so is aesthetically more correct. All told the simple Morinus System of Houses has much to recommend it.

Diagram 2: The Morinus House System and its House Boundaries at Birth.

———————— House Boundaries

— — — — Angular House Centres

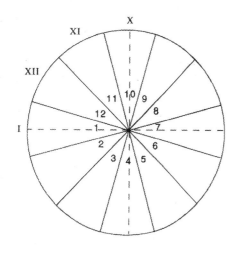

Figure 1 Distribution of House Boundaries About the Place of Birth

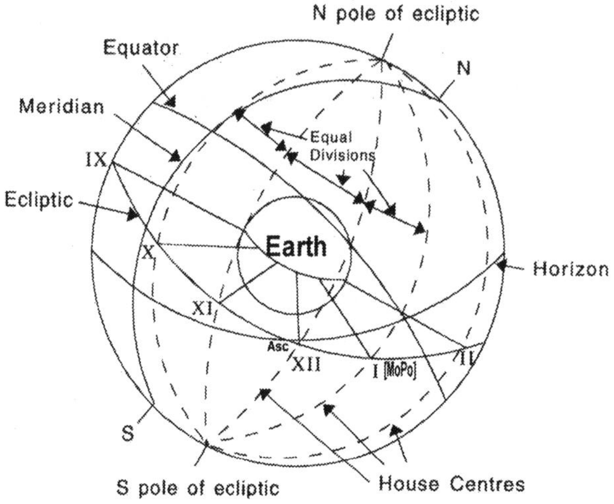

Figure 2 The Morinus House System[3]

As we have said, the twelve Houses chart the Earth's daily motion and describe our Earthly experience or "circumstances".

- -

CHAPTER 5

The Pre-Natal Epoch and the Ideal Birth Moment

Ancient teaching tells us that the Moon is the chief controller of human generation. Concerning our individual origins there are two moments, that of birth and that of fertilisation (epoch) that are important astrologically (see Chapter 1). The only astrological rules that come anywhere close to fitting the modern, genetic description of the birth process described there belong to the "Trutine of Hermes". These rules were developed primarily by Sepharial (W. Gorn-Old) and published in book form by Bailey as "The Pre-Natal Epoch" in 1916. The rules contain four variables: i.e. the positions of the Moon, of the Morin Point and, to a lesser extent, of the Sun as well as the sex of the baby-to-be. The rules state:

1) When the Moon at Birth is increasing in light (i.e. going from the new to the full Moon) it will be the Morin Point at Epoch, and the Moon at Epoch will be the Morin Point at Birth.

2) When the Moon at Birth is decreasing in light (i.e. going from the full to the new Moon) it will be the point opposite the Morin Point at Epoch, and the Moon at Epoch will be the point opposite the Morin Point at Birth.

These were extended by two observations:

a) When the Moon at Birth is increasing in light and below the Morin Point, or when decreasing in light and above the Morin Point, then the period of gestation is longer than the average.

b) When the Moon at Birth is increasing in light and above the Morin Point, or when decreasing in light and below the Morin Point, then the period of gestation is shorter than the average.

From these rules we can define Four Orders of Regular Epochs as follows in the Table:

Order	Condition	Period of Gestation
1	Moon above and increasing	273 days – x
2	Moon above and decreasing	273 days + x
3	Moon below and increasing	273 days + x
4	Moon below and decreasing	273 days – x

- -

273 days corresponds to the normal period of gestation (ten cycles of the Moon) counted backwards from the date of birth and gives us the "Index date". x is the number of days equivalent to the number of degrees of the Moon with respect to the Morin Point, or to its opposite, at birth, divided by 13. (On average the Moon travels 13^0 per day around the ecliptic [Zodiac]). Depending on the Order number, + or – x days from the Index date then gives the "Epoch date". There then follow three sex rules governing the positions of the Moon and of the Morin Point (both at Epoch) that allow us to determine the sex of the baby-to-be. Bailey's Table gives us the sex, or non-sex, of all the degrees of the Zodiac.

BAILEY'S SEX QUODRANTS

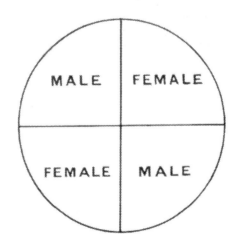

BAILEY'S TABLE OF SEX DEGREES

Sex	Limits of		Exact Sex Point	Limits of	
	Moon's Orb.	Morin Pt's Orb.		Morin Pt's Orb.	Moon's Orb.
F	—	—	♈ 0. 0	♈ 4.17	♈ 6.26
M	♈ 6.26	♈ 8.34	♈ 12.51	♈ 17. 9	♈ 19.17
M	♈ 19.17	♈ 21.26	♈ 25.43	♉ 0. 0	♉ 2. 9
F	♉ 2. 9	♉ 4.17	♉ 8.34	♉ 12.51	♉ 15. 0
M	♉ 15. 0	♉ 17. 9	♉ 21.26	♉ 25.43	♉ 27.51
F	♉ 27.51	♊ 0. 0	♊ 4.17	♊ 8.34	♊ 10.43
F	♊ 10.43	♊ 12.51	♊ 17. 9	♊ 21.26	♊ 23.34
F	♊ 23 34	♊ 25.43	♋ 0. 0	♋ 4.17	♋ 6.26
F	♋ 6.26	♋ 8.34	♋ 12.51	♋ 17. 9	♋ 19.17
M	♋ 19.17	♋ 21.26	♋ 25.43	♌ 0. 0	♌ 2. 9
M	♌ 2. 9	♌ 4.17	♌ 8.34	♌ 12.51	♌ 15. 0
M	♌ 15. 0	♌ 17. 9	♌ 21.26	♌ 25.43	♌ 27.51
M	♌ 27.51	♍ 0. 0	♍ 4.17	♍ 8.34	♍ 10.43
F	♍ 10.43	♍ 12.51	♍ 17. 9	♍ 21.26	♍ 23.34
M	♍ 23.34	♍ 25.43	♎ 0. 0	♎ 4.17	♎ 6.26
F	♎ 6.26	♎ 8.34	♎ 12.51	♎ 17. 9	♎ 19.17
F	♎ 19.17	♎ 21.26	♎ 25.43	♏ 0. 0	♏ 2. 9
M	♏ 2. 9	♏ 4.17	♏ 8.34	♏ 12.51	♏ 15. 0
F	♏ 15. 0	♏ 17. 9	♏ 21.26	♏ 25.43	♏ 27.51
M	♏ 27.51	♐ 0. 0	♐ 4.17	♐ 8.34	♐ 10.43
M	♐ 10.43	♐ 12.51	♐ 17. 9	♐ 21.26	♐ 23.34
M	♐ 23.34	♐ 25.43	♑ 0. 0	♑ 4.17	♑ 6.26
M	♑ 6.26	♑ 8.34	♑ 12.51	♑ 17. 9	♑ 19.17
F	♑ 19.17	♑ 21.26	♑ 25.43	♒ 0. 0	♒ 2. 9
F	♒ 2. 9	♒ 4.17	♒ 8.34	♒ 12.51	♒ 15. 0
F	♒ 15. 0	♒ 17. 9	♒ 21.26	♒ 25.43	♒ 27.51
F	♒ 27.51	♓ 0. 0	♓ 4.17	♓ 8.34	♓ 10.43
M	♓ 10.43	♓ 12.51	♓ 17. 9	♓ 21.26	♓ 23.34
F	♓ 23.34	♓ 25.43	♓ 30. 0	—	—

EXPLANATION.—Column 4 of the table shows the exact sex point. Cols 3 and 5 show where the influence of the Morin Pt. commences and finishes respectively. Cols. 2 and 6 show where the moon's influence commences and finishes respectively. Col. 1 gives the sex of the area between the longitudes in Cols. 2 and 6.

EXAMPLE.— Morin Pt at epoch, Cancer 18° 5'. Moon, Scorpio 15° 24'. Looking down the columns headed "Morin Pt.'s Orb," it will be seen that Cancer 18° 5' is outside the limits given. It is, therefore, negative. Looking down the columns headed "Moon's Orb," it will be seen that Scorpio 15° commences a female area, and the moon will therefore be in an area of that sex. The same rule applies to all cases.

For the Epoch Chart:-

1) When the Morin Point is negative (non-sex), as in strict regular and irregular epochs, the sex of the position occupied by the Moon will be the sex of the baby-to-be.

2) When the Moon and the Morin Point positions are within orbs of degrees of the same sex, the sex of the baby-to-be is the same as the positions so occupied.

3) When the Moon and the Morin Point positions are placed within orbs of degrees of the opposite sex – the Moon in a female position and the Morin Point in a male position, or vice-versa – the sex of the baby-to-be is determined by the sex of the quadrant containing the Moon.

The sex of a baby-to-be is decided at its moment of fertilisation by the invading sperm. In practice, and almost without exception, we know the sex of the child, and so we must find an Epoch that agrees with this.

The rules show that at the Pre-Natal Epoch (moment of fertilisation) there is a particular configuration of the heavens (mainly the Moon, but also the Sun) with respect to the Earth (Morin Point). It then follows, some nine months (ten cycles of the Moon) later, that there will be a related configuration of the heavens occurring at what we can call "The Ideal Birth Moment".

One reason for having the Ideal Birth Moment is to try to dispense with those influences at work to change the birth time so that it no longer occurs when it should. Major influences include induction by drugs, accidents (e.g. falling off a horse), the use of forceps, Caesarean births, breech births and the birth of a second, non-identical twin; but there must also be several, minor influences, all of which can lead to changed birth times. By contrast the moment of fertilisation (Pre-Natal Epoch) <u>in vivo</u> is highly sheltered, thermally constant and relatively uncomplicated compared with the process of birth, so that, potentially, it is a more reliable indicator of what the birth time should be. The problem here of course, is that we can't see when it happens.

Traditionally rectification is the process whereby we convert approximate or uncertain birth times into more accurate ones for correctly casting the horoscope. The use of the rules of the Pre-Natal Epoch for this purpose was claimed to be "the only reliable method of rectification". In the past astrologers regarded the moment of birth as sacrosanct, but realising how easily birth times can (be) change(d) perhaps we should regard the elaborate process of birth merely as a good indication of when a particular life on Earth begins, and that it simply is the best, so far, that nature can do. In other words, a life should begin when a particular configuration of the heavens with respect to the Earth occurs, and the actual birth moment, approximates, as closely as it can, to it. If we see the process of birth in this way, then rectification plays a far more important role, namely that of using the actual birth moment to determine what "The Ideal Birth Moment" should be.

The idea of the Pre-Natal Epoch is a consequence of the genetic nature of the whole birth process. Thus Addey has suggested, and recent results tend to confirm, that not only do we derive our physical form, but also our personalities from our genes, that have all become established and essentially unchangeable, at our moment of fertilisation. Now the interpretation of our horoscopes, cast for the dates, times and places of our moments of birth, also describes our personalities; i.e. the genetic traits already established at fertilisation must match those described at birth by interpretation of our horoscopes. This can only happen at one preordained time – the Ideal Birth Moment. We can conclude, despite the well-accepted view that our independent lives begin with our first breath that for each and every one of us, there is a natural, or ideal, time to be born. This personal and particular time is an important birthright, which we lose whenever our birth times no longer occur when they should, i.e. displaced by the influences already mentioned. Similarly, and topically, we become displaced from our "time" by cryoscopic preservation techniques, by the process of human cloning, as well as potentially "unfit" by indiscriminate injection of sperm into eggs.

CHAPTER 6

FIRST IMPRESSIONS

Planet Distribution, Overall Chart Shaping and Interplanetary Aspects.

To gain a first impression of a person we examine a chart's **Planetary Distribution:** For Northern hemisphere births the direction of the Equator is South so that the top of the page of the horoscope has this direction and its left-hand edge represents the East* (from where the Sun rises).

If most of the planets lie to the East in a chart then the interpretation is that destiny is in the person's own hands. If they lie to the West predominantly then the person's destiny is in others' hands or dependent on prevailing conditions. If most of the planets lie above the horizon (i.e. in the top half of the chart) then the interpretation is that the person is mostly objective (concerned with practical and visible things). Conversely, if they lie mostly below the horizon (i.e. in the bottom half of the chart) then the interpretation is

- -

*For Southern Hemisphere births the Equator's direction is North, so that the top of the page now stands for this direction and its right-hand edge represents the East. Thus the horoscope for the Southern hemisphere is a mirror image of that of the Northern one about the M.C. – I.C. axis (i.e. one half rotation about this axis). The House System we use in the Northern Hemisphere in this book is that due to Morinus; its counterpart we could use for the Southern Hemisphere is called the Zariel Axial Rotation House System.

that the person is largely subjective (i.e. concerned mostly with spiritual and invisible/abstract things).

For our next impression of the person we examine a chart's **Overall Shaping:** Of more specific use than the planetary distribution, the interpretation of the overall planetary chart shaping has been considered only relatively recently. Seven basic types occur:

1) <u>The Splash.</u> The planets are scattered around the chart. At best this reveals a person with a genuine, universal width of interest, or, at worst, one who scatters his/her interests too much. The 'scattered' souls of life are largely met in connection with 'scattered' situations. Scatter is fundamental in their nature. Theirs is a(n) (un)witting and (un)fortunate contribution to change and reconstruction that, actually, is an everyday part of reality.

2) <u>The Bundle.</u> All the person's planets are concentrated within a third of a chart. This indicates that the course of the life is restricted within certain narrow bands of opportunity; i.e. one who is inhibited compared, say, with a 'Splash' type person.

3) <u>The Locomotive.</u> This is reverse of the 'Bundle' in that all the person's planets are confined within two thirds of a chart, leaving the remaining third empty. Here the temperament drives forwards; the important planet is that leading in a clockwise direction towards the empty third and is judged by the House which it occupies. The person's strong sense of deprivation, or need, appears as a problem to be solved, or a task to be achieved in the social and intellectual world around that person. The temperament is a self-driving one, an executive eccentricity that is neither odd nor unbalanced but powerful. The locomotive shows a dynamic and exceptional practical capacity, which is moved more by external factors in the environment than by aspects of the person's own character.

4) <u>The Bowl.</u> All the planets lie in one half of the chart. If the division is along the horizon, or along the meridian line, a hemisphere of influence is formed. The occupied half shows the person's activity and organisation whereas the unoccupied half becomes a challenge to existence, or the need and emptiness to which the person must direct his/her attention. What the person contains is contrasted by what the person lacks and causes the advocacy of some cause, the furtherance of a mission, or an introspective concern over the purpose of existence. The 'Bowl' type has something to give to his/her fellows, literally or psychologically, constructively or vindictively, because the person's world arises from division, i.e. frustration and uncertainty. The bowl person is self-expending or self-seeking and more practically interested in what things mean as well as in what they are. The 'bowl' tends to 'scoop up' things when the leading planet lies to the East, or to 'capture' things (i.e. consummate various life phases) when it lies to the West. This type of person tends to be idealistic.

5) <u>The Bucket.</u> All the planets but one lie in one hemisphere. This one planet constitutes the 'Bucket's' handle. When it is alone, either above the horizon or below, or either to the East or to the West, then it is known as a 'singleton' and reveals an important direction of interest. A vertical handle approximates a fanhandle pattern (see aspect patterns, later) and the direction of energies is intensified. When the handle is situated 'clockwise' the person leans towards caution, or self-conscious preparedness, generally; when it lies 'anticlockwise' the person is more impulsive, or inclined to respond to an immediate, rather than future, promise. There is a particular and rather uncompromising direction to the person's life-effort. The person adapts his allegiances to lines along which he can make his

efforts count for the most. The 'Bucket' type reveals a real instructor and inspirer of others at best, but at worst the agitator and malcontent. It shows a person who dips deeply into life and pours forth the gathered experiences of the his/her life with unremitting zeal.

6) <u>The See-Saw.</u>   The planets lie in two groups, roughly opposed to each other across the chart. The person's tendency here is to act at all times under a consideration of opposing views, or under a sensitiveness to contrasting and antagonistic possibilities. The person exists in a world of conflicts, of definite polarities but is capable of unique achievement through a development of unsuspected relations in life, although s/he is apt to waste his/her energies through his/her improper alignment with various situations. This type of person tends to be indecisive, but choices finally made will have been well-considered.

7) <u>The Splay.</u> The planets cluster together in strong and sharp aggregations at irregular points around the chart that suggests a unique individual with purposeful life emphases. The disposition juts out into experience according to his/her own very special tastes. The person makes his/her own anchorage in existence that is marked by a robust resistance to pigeon-holing, either in the neat, conventional components of nature, or within the idea compartments of his/her associates. This type of person shows a splay-foot certainty in every approach s/he makes to the problems of life. The 'Splay' reveals a very intense personality who cannot be limited to any single, steady point of application. The temperament is inclined to be particular and impersonal in his/her interests, in contrast with the universal and impersonal set of the 'Splash' and the particular and personal set of the 'Bundle' types.

The planetary chart shapings, which the charts reveal, help a person to direct his or her life-style confidently, which is the main justification for the practice and study of Natal Astrology.

Before embarking on our interpretation process more fully we need to examine and appreciate the Aspect Grid component of our charts. Once again the computer program has found all the aspects, thereby saving us considerable time and effort but the program only supplies us with what we have asked it for.

Aspects are specific angles (i.e. the Zodiac circle of 360^0 divided by successive whole numbers starting with one), subtended at the centre of the Earth, between two planets. They are measured in degrees around the Zodiac (Ecliptic). For example, division of 360^0 by one gives us 360^0, which brings us back to where we started from on the circle, making an angle of 0^0, i.e. two planets appearing to occupy the same position, which we call the conjunction. Division by two gives us 180^0 and places a planet diametrically across the ecliptic circle from our starting point, thereby giving us the opposition. Similarly, division by three results in 120^0, giving us the trine, and division by four gives us the square, an aspect of 90^0, and so on.

There are five major aspects and several minor ones:

Major Aspect Name	Angular Distance around Ecliptic.	Aspect Orb	Symbol	Nature
CONJUNCTION	0^0	8^0	☌	Variable
OPPOSITION	180^0	8^0	☍	Difficulty
TRINE	120^0	8^0	△	Ease
SQUARE	90^0	8^0	□	Difficulty
SEXTILE	60^0	4^0	✳	Ease

Minor Aspect Family Name	Angular Distance around Ecliptic	Aspect Orb	Symbol	Nature
Quintile	72^0, 144^0	2^0	Q, Q2	Intelligence
Septile	51^0 26', 102^0 54' 154^0 18'.	2^0	S, S2,S3	Independence
Semi Square	45^0	2^0	∠	Difficulty
Sesquiquadrate	135^0	2^0	⊡	Difficulty
Nonile	40^0, 80^0, 160^0.	2^0	N, N2,N4	Ease
Decile	36^0, 108^0.	2^0	D, D3	Intelligence
Undecile	32^0 43' etc.	2^0	U, U2 etc.	Gentility
Semi-sextile	30^0	2^0	⋎	Ease
Quincunx	150^0	2^0	⊼	Difficulty

We need to learn the symbols because they are used universally by astrologers but this is helped by practice. Aspect interpretation is important because it qualifies the way in which the principles of the planets manifest. Thus the meaning of every aspect is 'two-way'.

Aspects to the Ruler, Sun or Moon are usually more important. Traditionally a planet within 3^0 of the Sun was said to be 'combust', i.e. made incapable of operating characteristically because it was over-powered by the Sun's influence but, on the other hand, it may indicate a close identity between the person's will and the principle of the planet concerned. This situation applies particularly to Mercury. Because Mercury and the Sun always appear close to each other in the skies (never more than 28^0 apart) the 'mentality' is always close to the central 'will'; sometimes ahead and then it falls behind. This Sun/Mercury relationship shows four types of mentality: When Mercury is ahead, or rising ahead of the Sun (i.e. behind in the Zodiac!) then the person's mind is "eager". If it is more than 14^0 ahead, i.e. more than half its possible distance, it is also "untrammelled". If it is ahead by less than 14^0 the mind is eager but more will-censored or self-conscious. When Mercury rises behind the Sun (i.e. ahead in the Zodiac!) by more than 14^0 the mind is "deliberate" rather than eager but is untrammelled. However, when Mercury rises behind the Sun by less than 14^0 the mind is still deliberate but also self-conscious. Possibly we could extend this kind of argument to Sun/Venus situations (they never appear more than 48^0 apart) or even to Venus/Mercury ones (they never appear more than 76^0 apart) but these have never appeared to be useful.

Additionally, other aspects to two aspecting planets modify the interpretation of the original aspect. Aspects not only unite planets, they emphasise the sign (if conjunction), the element (if trine) and the quality (if opposition or square) in which it functions. Traditionally they were described as good or bad, or evil but now words such as easy and difficult are preferred. The nature of an aspect depends on the planets making up the aspect. Venus and Jupiter tend to be beneficial/easy whereas Saturn and Mars make the aspects difficult. An exact aspect is very much stronger than a wide one. The extreme width of its action is called its 'orb' i.e. the Orb of an aspect is the distance of separation permitted by the planets while in aspect. Further considerations include the absence of aspects to a planet (its principle is then not well-co-ordinated with the rest of the personality) and aspects between two planets that are not aspected by any of the others (the personality may then seem to be divided or split). When two planets, not in proper aspect to each other, are both aspected by a third, this other may bring them into aspect by "translation of light". When each of two planets is found to be in the sign ruled by the other they are brought into a relationship as if they were in conjunction. This is called "Mutual Reception". A planet moving towards exactness of aspect with another is said to be "applying" and so strengthening, whereas if it is moving away then it is called "separating" and so weakening. If two planets are equidistant from the celestial equator, either to its North or to its South, or both, then they are said to be in "Parallel of Declination", symbol P, with an orb of 1^0. If on the same side of the Earth then P has the property of the conjunction but if on the opposite side then P's property is of the opposition. Ps are very rarely used. 'Noniles' and 'Undeciles' (the ecliptic divided by nine and eleven respectively) have not been used at all.

In deciding whether a given aspect will work out in terms of character or destiny it is suggested that so far as character is concerned, contradictory influences tend, as life advances and the character becomes formed, to cancel out. As the nature becomes stabilised, characteristics that are least compatible with the needs of the environment, will die away. However, planetary effects, denied release in terms of character, tend to manifest in terms of the external life (destiny) such as in health, finance, reputation, etc.

With the foregoing discussion about aspects in mind we need to set the computer program to provide us with no more than a satisfactory minimum number of aspects and their respective 'orbs'. The program supplies us automatically with the degree of separation from exactness and whether the aspect is applying or separating. We shall use aspects based on the division of the Zodiac by the numbers 1, 2, 3, 4, 5, 6, 8 and 12 and no more* with the orbs given in the tables. Not only does the computer program generate the Aspect Grid it also provides us with a pattern of aspect lines between the planets in the centre of the chart. Red lines have been used for 'easy' aspects, blue lines for 'difficult' ones and dashed, black lines for minor aspects.

This practice is of great help and enables planetary patterns to be seen at a glance.

Specific Interplanetary Aspect Patterns: To make sure we identify all of these we need to examine charts carefully. Presently there are six main groups:-

1) <u>T-Square:</u> The tenseness of an opposition will be aggravated when another planet is square to both ends of the opposition (bi-square). Usually a T-Square is of the cardinal, fixed or mutable quality. The short arm of the T (or the bi-square planet) gives the T-Square its focus. On the other hand the tenseness will be eased if another planet is trine to one end of the opposition and at the same time sextile to the other. This is called mediation. We need to give special attention to the 'quality' in which the square and opposition fall.

a) Those in cardinal signs are apt to cause abrupt and complete changes in the activities and ways of thought.

b) Those in fixed signs often lie dormant for long periods but act drastically when they do act. In some respects these are the least difficult of the three classes.

- -

*Division of the Zodiac by 7 has been proposed. It is the only digit not exactly divisible into 360°. The result is 51.'428571'; the last six numbers are recurring. Numerologically, a recurring decimal represents an interchangeability of levels and the septile aspect perhaps indicates an ability to change levels (i.e. undergo transformation). It may have an effect of an intangible, or spiritual nature since 7 is the number of Neptune.

c) Those in mutable signs denote vacillation and indecision; health is affected and accidents occur. They are the most troublesome of the three classes.

2) <u>Grand Trine:</u> The ease of working of an element (fire, earth, air, water) is intensified when three or more planets complete an equilateral triangle in the chart. Sometimes the ease produced can lead some persons to become "parasitical".

3) <u>Grand Cross:</u> Difficulty is raised to an optimum when four or more planets complete a four-cornered square that will simultaneously contain two oppositions. Charts containing this pattern should be examined for mediation, e.g. the presence of an easing aspect to one of the four corners. Crosses formed in different qualities are different in effect. Thus a cardinal cross implies an intention to surmount difficulties, a fixed one to put up with them and a mutable one to by-pass them, but all of these lead to resultant strain for the person.

4) <u>Yod – The Finger of God:</u> The pattern of two planets in close sextile, with a third in quincunx to both, is called a Yod. This suggests opportunities that the person seemingly is compelled to take up, for better or worse, depending on the rest of the chart. There is always transformation contained in the basic working out of the Yod. As we can imagine there are other triangular patterns similar to the Yod. For example, two planets in close square, with a third that is sesquiquadrate to both; or two planets in close quintile with a third that is biquintile to both. Interpretations for these will be different from those of the Yod.

5) <u>Bi-Aspect patterns:</u> A third planet at a specific midpoint between two others tends to form meaningful triangles. Such planets are said to be bi-an aspect, such as bi-sextile (at the midpoint of a

trine); bi-semisextile (at the midpoint of a sextile) and bi-semisquare (at the midpoint of a square).

6) <u>Kites:</u> The starting condition for a kite is an opposition that is then flanked equidistantly and specifically, on either side, by other planets. Thus a Grand Cross is one extreme form of kite that contains optimum strain. At the other extreme, one planet opposing a closely gathered group of planets (i.e. a stellium) across a chart produces a fanhandle. If we find a Grand Trine with an extra planet that is bi-sextile on one side then this planet will oppose the remaining planet(s) across the chart and so we form a Grand Trine Kite. This is the kite that contains the greatest amount of ease. Similarly, if we take a Yod and find an extra planet that is bi-semisextile to those forming the sextile we see that it will also oppose the remaining planet that is quincunx to both those forming the sextile. This kite contains considerable strain. Kites based on the quintile and decile families probably also contain significant strain. The Table summarises the presently accepted types of possible kites:

Kite Name	Family	Angle subtended at the Earth by the short cross-bar.	Influence
Fanhandle	Conjunction	Essentially 0^0	Strain
Quincunx (Yod)	Dodecile	60^0	Strain + Ease
Biquintile	Decile	72^0	Neutral + Strain
Sesquiquadrate	Octile	90^0	Increased Strain
Trine (Grand)	Sextile	120^0	More Ease than Strain
Tredecile	Quintile	144^0	Neutral + Strain
Square (Grand +)	Quadruplicity	180^0	Optimum Strain

The meaning of a kite, in general, is that the principles of the planets comprising the kite will all be well-integrated within the character of the person involved. Notice that all kites contain innate strain due to the opposition produced by the kite's long cross-bar. The amount of strain is then modified by the nature of the other aspects making-up the kite as shown in the Table. Relief or aggravation of strain can also be achieved by external easing or straining aspects to the ends of the cross-bars. The main focus of a kite occurs at the sharp end apart from a Grand Cross kite, which doesn't have a sharp end; we then need other factors to help to decide the focus of this kind of kite (e.g. Sun, Moon or Ruler, or that planet at the Morin Point or M.C.).

Occasionally we encounter a chart that contains a huge number of aspects and the suggestion here is that although the character will be well-integrated it seems that too much can be going on for the person to know what to do for the best. This, of course, presents a challenge for Astrology. Conversely, some charts contain relatively few aspects suggesting that the planetary principles are not well-integrated within the character thereby leading perhaps to problems of social acceptance for the person. Here we have another challenge for Astrology.

Three Other Common Factors:*

☊☊ The Dragon's head (Moon's Ascending Node) is a point of general "protection".

☋ The Dragon's tail (Moon's Descending Node) is a point of general "self-undoing".

⊕ The Part of Fortune (Morin Point – The Moon + the Sun) is a point of general "self-interest".

- -

*For our present purposes we shall not consider 'points-in-space' like these. The only point-in-space that will concern us here is the Morin Point

52

that fixes the orientation of the sky with respect to the Earth at our moment of birth/epoch. Even then we shall confine our attention only to interpreting its sign and decanate briefly and then move on to interpreting the sign and House positions of their respective rulers together only with the most important aspects that each receives.

- -

CHAPTER 7

Producing Natal* Charts Using a Computer

"Happiness is doing something that matters."
Sister Wendy, *The One Show*, BBC 1, 2010.

* Henceforward, natal can stand for either or both birth and epoch.

1) <u>Producing the Initial Birth Chart:</u> There are three pieces of data that we require to produce a birth chart: namely the time, date and place of birth. With these to hand, switch on the computer and double left click on the Astrological Software Icon on the Desktop to bring the program's Opening Screen up onto the Monitor. The 'Current Settings' Box occupies the top half of the screen (see picture).

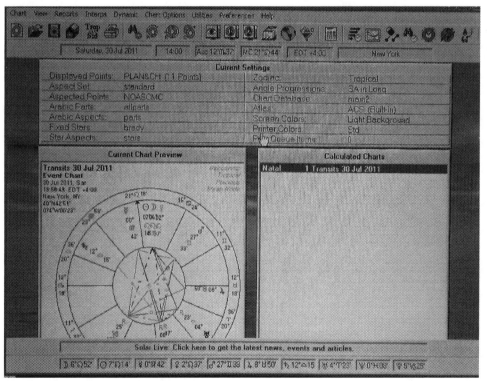

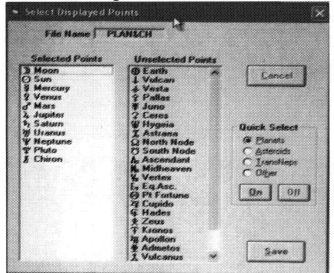

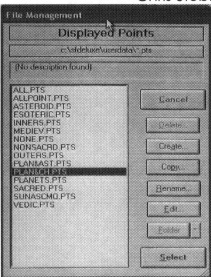

2)   <u>Programming the 'Current Settings' Box:</u>   Click on 'Displayed Points', then click on 'Select' and 'Planet and Chart Points' in the resulting 'File Management' Box and click on Edit. The 'Select Displayed Points' Box appears. Simply 'Quick Select' Planets by clicking inside the small white circle alongside to include Moon, Sun, Mercury, Venus, Mars up to and including Pluto. In the 'Unselected Points' List select Chiron and then click on 'On'. Then click on Save.

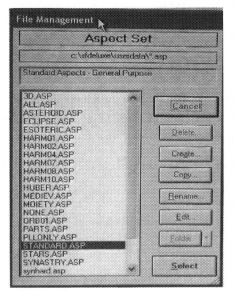

We have now selected all our required 11 'Displayed Points'.

Return now to the 'Current Settings' Box on the opening screen and click on 'Aspect Set' to bring up the File Management 'Aspect Set' Box. Click on Edit so that the 'Edit Aspect Set' Box appears. Click on 'Enable' for the first 11 aspects from Conjunction to Biquintile inclusively. By clicking on each aspect in turn set all the 'Natal Orb' Boxes for the

55

Conjunction, Opposition, Trine and Square boxes to 8⁰ 00'. For the Sextile set all these boxes to 4⁰ 00' and similarly we set all the Quintile and BiQuintile 'Natal Orb' Boxes to 3⁰ 00'. The 'Prog' and 'Tran Orb' Boxes refer to techniques of Prediction and don't concern us here. Finally click on Save and then on 'Cancel' twice to remove the last two boxes.

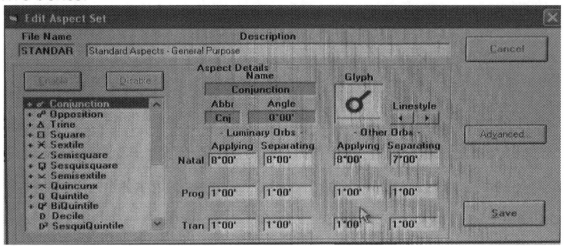

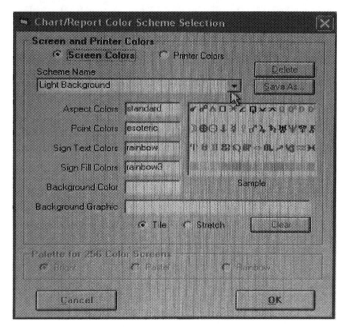

Return once more to the 'Current Settings' Box and click on 'Aspected Points' to bring up the appropriate 'File Management' Box. Select 'NOASCMC.ADP', click 'Cancel' and so return again to the 'Current Settings' Box. We leave the next eight items listed and click on 'Screen Colours' to bring up the 'Chart/Report Colour Scheme Selection' Box. The Picture shows a commonly chosen set of colours for the Screen, which we repeat for the printer.   Below the 'Current Settings' Box on the Opening Screen we see a 'Current Chart Preview' Box to the left and alongside to the right we find the corresponding 'Calculated Chart' Box. The 'Current Chart Preview' Box shows all our current settings for the 'Transits of the Day', which we shall ignore.

3) <u>Producing an Initial Birth Chart:</u> Click on the far left 'New Chart', blue circle icon underneath 'Chart' at the top of the 'Opening Screen'. This brings up the 'New Chart Data Entry' Box that we have filled in for Diana-Princess of Wales.

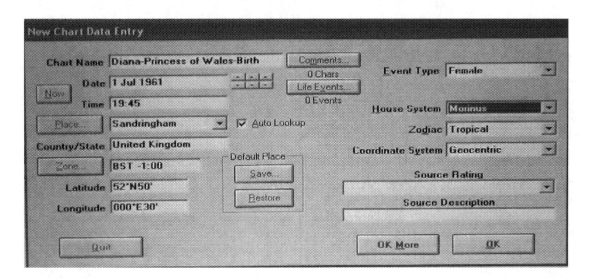

Clicking on OK returns us to the Opening Screen where the 'Current Chart Preview' Box shows Diana's Chart and the 'Calculated Charts' box highlights 'Diana, Princess-of-Wales Birth. We notice that by 'Zone' British Summer Time (BST) of one hour has been subtracted from the birth time. By using the 'Auto-Lookup' function the Latitude and Longitude of Sandringham become entered immediately after we have typed in the 'Place' and 'Country/State' Boxes. Obviously the Event type is for a female birth; we select Morinus as our 'House System'; the 'Zodiac' is Tropical and our 'Coordinate System' is Geocentric. Clicking on 'OK' returns us automatically to the Opening Screen where we see that the 'Current Chart Preview' Box displays Diana's Birth Chart and the 'Calculated Charts' Box confirms that it is her chart that is being displayed. By clicking on Transits in this box we bring back the initially displayed Transits chart into the 'Current Chart Preview' Box. We return to Diana's chart again by clicking on Diana in the 'Calculated Charts' Box.

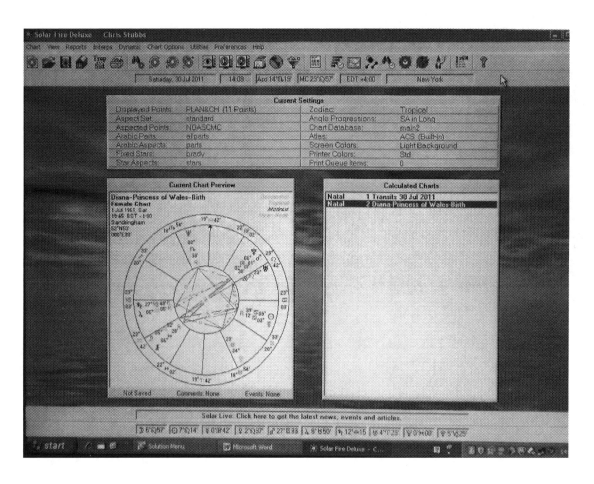

Click now on 'View' right next to 'Chart' at the top left of the Opening Screen to release a drop-down menu. We click on 'Current Chart' to bring up a full screen display of Diana's initial Birth Chart:

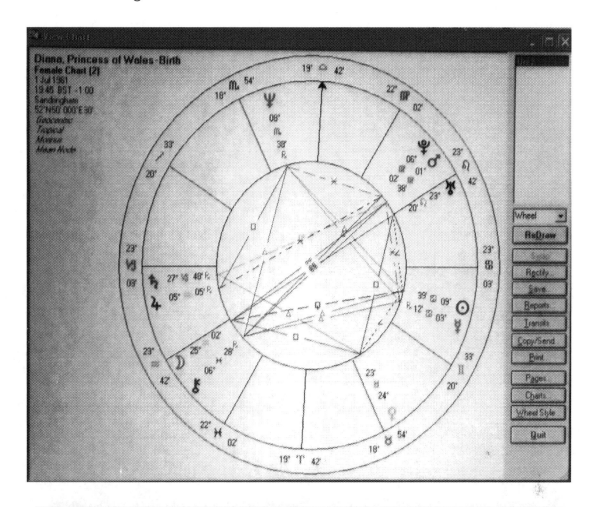

On the right we click on the 'Print' Box to bring up the 'Print Current Image' Box. We can select either the 'Colour/Grey Scale' or the 'Black only' option and then click on 'Print' to obtain our desired 'hard-copy' of Diana's Birth Chart from the printer. This type of chart is useful to help us find Index and Epoch dates. Alternatively we can click on 'Current Chart and Grid' on the View Drop-Down menu to bring up a full-screen display of 'Diana's Birth Chart and Aspect Grid':

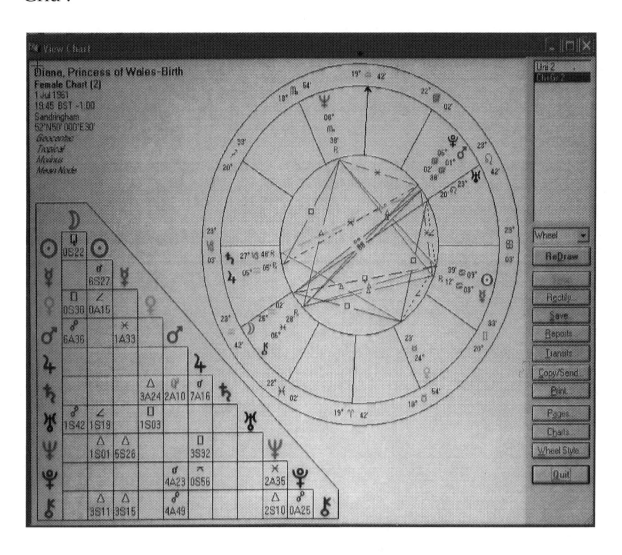

Once again, clicking on 'Print' brings up the 'Print Current Image' Box from which we can obtain our desired 'hard copy' of Diana's Birth Chart and Aspect Grid' as before. We shall find that this type of chart is useful when assembling a person's interpretations.

4) <u>Finding Diana's Index Date:</u> The purpose of finding the Index date is to make the job of finding the Epoch date that much easier. It has no other real value.

We click on the 'New Chart' Icon again to bring the 'New Chart Data Entry' Box back that still contains Diana's birth data. The Index date occurs 10 cycles of the Moon (about 9 months) earlier than the birth date on the day when the Moon occupied the same position as it did at birth. In the first entry box we change the word 'birth' to 'index'. The second entry box now needs to contain the Index date. The easiest way to effect this is to correct the birth month to that 3 months ahead and then the birth year to the previous one, except when the monthly change increases the birth year by one (i.e. as it does when it is Oct, Nov or Dec), in which case the birth year is left unchanged. In Diana's case the second entry box now reads 1 Oct 1960. The time entry box is now changed to read 00:00, i.e. the time at midnight at the start of the Index day. Now we click on OK, which returns us to the opening screen where the 'Current Chart Preview' Box displays the provisional Index date chart. As the Moon travels 13^0 on average every day through the Zodiac (by contrast the Sun only travels through 1^0 and the Morin Point through 360^0) we see that the Moon indeed occupies its birth position on the 1st Oct. 1960 at about 15:00. This then is Diana's Index date. Generally the Index date always occurs within 3 days of exactly nine months before the Birth date and so it is an easy matter to find it, but this hasn't been necessary for Diana's case.   Now let's use the Index date to find Diana's Epoch date.

5) <u>Finding Diana's Epoch data:</u> On the Opening Screen and in the 'Calculated Chart' Box click on Diana's birth chart to bring it back to the 'Current Chart Preview' Box.   We need to note four things. Firstly we see that the Moon is below the Earth (i.e. beneath the Morin Point – Opposite-to-the-Morin-Point Axis).   Secondly we see that it is decreasing in light from the Full Moon (that occurs when the Moon lies directly opposite to the Sun) to the New Moon (that occurs when the Moon lies in conjunction with the Sun).   This means that Diana's Epoch will be 4th Order (see Chapter 4).   Thirdly, by referring to Bailey's Table of Sex degrees, we observe that the Moon occupies a Female position at 25⁰ Aquarius and, fourthly, so does the Morin Point at 23⁰ Capricorn.   This means that the Epoch is a Sex one that, in turn, means that, potentially, there are three valid Epochs for a girl birth.   One of these Epochs shows that both the Morin Point and the Moon occupy Female positions and so must constitute a valid Epoch for Diana.   Let us examine this possibility first.   Following Bailey, it will be the Irregular, 3rd Variation one.

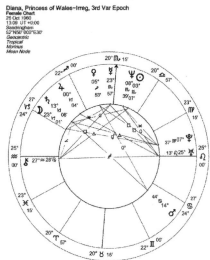

Diana, Princess of Wales—Irreg, 3rd Var Epoch
Female Chart
26 Oct 1960
13:09 UT +0:00
Sandringham
52°N50' 000°E30'
Geocentric
Tropical
Morinus
Mean Node

We count the degrees from the Moon at birth in the 2nd House round to the Opposite of the Morin Point and then continue over the Earth to the Morin Point, altogether some 320⁰.   We divide this by 13 to give us about 25 days.   Thus the Epoch will lie within the 28 days following the Index date and will occur on the day when the Moon reaches the same Zodiacal position as the Morin Point at birth (i.e. 23⁰

Capricorn). We click on the 'New Chart' Icon to bring back the 'New Chart Data Entry' Box. After changing 'Index' to 'Epoch' we examine the chart at midnight at the start of the 26th October, 1960. Now we determine the time of day on this day when the Moon's Zodiacal position at birth (25^0 Aquarius) becomes the Morin Point at Epoch. This happens at 13:09 on the 26th October, 1960. Interestingly we note that the sex of the Moon's quadrant is male, which suggests that that the other two possible Epochs will also show that the Moon occupies a male quadrant thereby rendering them invalid as Epochs for a girl birth, but we shall need to confirm this*

- -

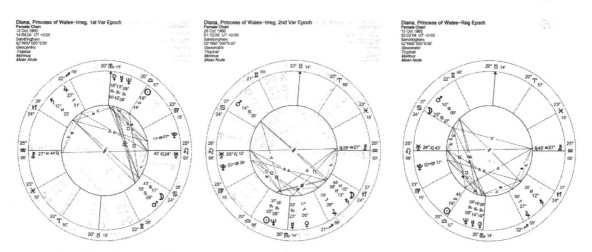

*Following Bailey we count from the Moon to the Opposite of the Morin Point, i.e. some 148^0, that divided by 13 corresponds roughly to 11 days. Adding this to the Index date of the 1st October gives us the 12th October, 1960, the date for the possible Irregular, 1st Variation Epoch. We now find the time on this day when the Moon's birth position (25^0 Aquarius) occupies the Morin Point. For this possible Epoch we know that the Morin Point's position is female, the Moon's position is male and we see that the Moon indeed occupies a male quadrant, thus invalidating this Epoch for a girl birth.

The Irregular, 2nd Variation Epoch also occurs on the 26th October, 1960. This time we determine the time on this day when the Moon's birth position (25⁰ Aquarius) occupies the position of the Opposite of the Morin Point. This happens at 01:11 and means that the Morin Point will occupy a male position. The Moon at this time (19⁰ Aquarius) occupies a female position but the sex of the quadrant occupying the Moon is male, making the Epoch invalid for a future girl birth.

The fourth and final possibility, the Regular Epoch, cannot constitute a valid Epoch for a girl birth because both the Moon and Morin Point occupy male positions. Therefore the only possible Epoch leading to a girl birth is the Irregular, 3rd Variation one, which we examined first.

- -

6) <u>Matching Diana's Epoch and Birth Charts:</u> According to the rules of the Pre-Natal Epoch we take the position of the Moon at Epoch and find when this position occupies the Morin Point on the day of birth. In fact the agreement between these two is remarkably good and it will take us but a few moments to match the Epoch and Birth charts accurately. Thus we find that Diana's Ideal Birth Time occurs at 19:44:52 on the 1st July, 1961, just 8 seconds behind the time given. The time for the matched Epoch is 13:09:08 on the 26th October, 1960. Note that not only does the Moon's position at Epoch match that of the Morin Point at Birth but that the Moon's position at Birth also matches the Morin Point at Epoch. Now we print-off these two charts together with their aspect grids. We shall use these charts to derive Diana's character and so determine her own particular version of 'Heaven's Message'. For now we return to the 'Calculated Charts' box, highlight all of Diana's charts and delete them ready to replace them with those for Theodore Roosevelt (TR), 26th President of the United States.

7) <u>Finding TR's Index date:</u> We click on the 'New Chart' Icon again to bring up the 'New Chart Data Entry' box and replace

Diana's birth data with that of TR*. Clicking OK returns us to the Opening Screen where TR's birth chart is displayed in the 'Current Chart Preview' Box.

To find TR's Index date we replace 27th Oct by 27th Jan but for this case, leave the year unchanged As for Diana we have changed 'birth' to 'index' in the first entry box and now change the time in the third entry box to 00:00. We click on OK to show us the 'Current Chart Preview' box displaying the chart for midnight at the start of the Index date. We see that on this day (about 15:20) the Moon occupies the same position as it did at birth so that, once again, we have found the Index date straight away.

8) <u>Finding TR's Epoch data:</u> Now we click on TR's birth chart in the 'Calculated Charts' box to bring his birth chart back to the 'Current Chart Preview' box. As for Diana we need to make the same four observations for TR as we did for her birth chart. We see that

---

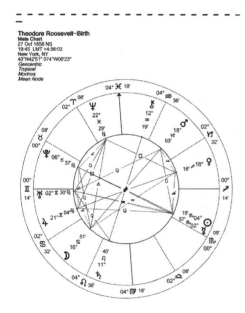

Theodore Roosevelt~Birth
Male Chart
27 Oct 1858 NS
19:45 LMT +4:56:02
New York, NY
40°N42'51" 074°W00'23"
Geocentric
Tropical
Morinus
Mean Node

*Previously TR's birth chart was derived from the time of 11:45 given by TR himself to George J McCormack. Here TR's birth time is taken as 19:45, as reported by his maternal grandmother (Mrs Martha Bullock) by letter to a friend the following day after TR's birth, which, reportedly, was an easy one. There appears to be some attempt at accuracy here. Perhaps G J McCormack misheard TR, confusing 11:45 a.m. with 7:45 p.m. Because the charts deriving from Mrs Bullock's time fit him rather well, as we shall soon see, we have used her birth time here.

the Moon lies below the Morin Point and that it is decreasing in light so that the TR's Epoch, like Diana's, will be 4th Order. Similarly, the positions of the Moon and of the Morin Point are female meaning that we have a Sex Epoch but opposite in sex to that of TR. In turn, and once again, this means that there are three potentially valid Epochs for TR's birth. One of these, showing both the Morin Point and the Moon's positions to be male at Epoch, will provide a valid Epoch for a boy birth.

Following Bailey, this will be the Regular Epoch. We determine this by counting from the Moon in the 2nd House to the Opposite to the Morin Point, some 133°, corresponding to 10 days roughly. Therefore this Epoch will occur on the 6th February, 1858, on which day we need to find when the Moon's position at birth becomes the position of the Opposite of the Morin Point i.e. at about 03:57. Interestingly we see that the Moon, at 22° 36' Scorpio, occupies a male quadrant, indicating that the other two possible Epochs, showing the same situation, also could well be valid for a boy birth, although we shall now confirm this.

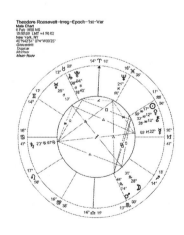

For the Irregular, 1st Variation Epoch we find the time on the 6th February, 1858 when the Moon's position at birth (16° Cancer) is occupied by the Morin Point. This occurs at 15:55 when the Moon lies at 28° 31' Scorpio. For this possible Epoch we see that the Morin Point's position is female; the Moon's position is male and the Moon's quadrant is male making this a valid Epoch for a boy birth as well.

Following Bailey, for the possible Irregular, 2nd Variation Epoch (right) we count the degrees from the Moon at birth in the 2nd House to the Opposite of the Morin Point and then round over the Earth to the Morin Point (313⁰). This number divided by 13 gives the number of days after the Index date, i.e. 24 for this Epoch's occurrence on the 20th February, 1858. We now find the time (03:02) on this day

when the Morin Point occupies the opposite of the position of the Moon at birth, i.e. 16⁰ Capricorn. For this possible Epoch we see that the position of the Morin Point is male and that the Moon's position is female but that the quadrant containing the Moon is male meaning that this too is a valid Epoch for a boy birth.

Finally, the Irregular 3rd Variation Epoch (below) that also occurs on the 20th February 1858 shows that at 15:00 the Morin Point's position (16⁰ Cancer) and the Moon's position (29⁰ Taurus) are both female. Even though the quadrant containing the Moon is male we see that this Epoch cannot constitute a valid one for a boy birth. Thus we are left with three potentially valid Epochs for TR's birth: the Regular, the Irregular 1st Variation and the Irregular 2nd Variation. The Irregular 1st Variation Epoch generates an Ideal Birth time that is closest to the reported one. It also places retrograde Uranus close to the Morin Point. Moreover, Saturn rising in Cancer at Epoch is the one that can explain TR's

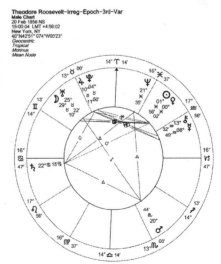

strange quirks, both in vocal expression and also in physical form. The Irregular Epoch 2nd Variation has no aspect between the Sun and Mars to help to explain TR's drive and achievement. The Regular Epoch, with all three factors occupying male positions, has the Sun square to Mars, as does the Irregular 1st Variation one, but, without retrograde Saturn rising, fails to describe him convincingly. On balance the latter Epoch describes him much better and so we shall select this one as being TR's correct Epoch.

   9) <u>Matching TR's Epoch and Birth Charts</u>: Because the Moon at Epoch lies at 28° 31' Scorpio, the Morin Point at birth needs to occupy the opposite position of 28° 31' Taurus. Following a short iteration procedure we find that the Ideal Birth Time occurs at 19:38, some seven minutes before the reported one. We shall use this chosen Irregular 1st Variation Epoch – Ideal Birth Time combination of charts

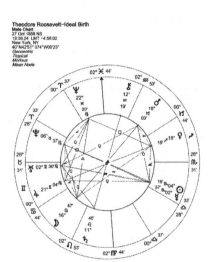

to determine TR's character and so his version of 'Heaven's Message'. Finally, we return to the 'Calculated Charts' box, highlight all the charts there and delete them before exiting the program.

   Following Diana's and TR's examples, we see that occasionally there will be persons for whom there could well be three valid Epochs for their given birth time. As the three Epochs are Sex ones in which the sex of the quadrant containing the Moon will be the same as their own, they will all be valid potentially, but only one will be the correct one. Different from the corresponding, closely similar birth charts that each one generates, the potentially valid Epochs differ significantly in time. This means that their interpretations will be significantly different. Possibly we can identify the correct one simply by examining the interpretation of their Morin Points and planets rising and deciding which one fits best, as we have just done for TR. If this proves insufficient then we can consider the Sun-Moon polarities both by Sign and by House. These should reveal significant differences. To try to avoid errors, we may be able to identify medical, physical appearance or psychological differences. Finally, a first birth could suggest a longer gestation period than usual, a third or fourth birth a shorter one, or we could opt for the one closest to the average gestation period of nine months, if all else fails.

- -

CHAPTER 8

Interpretation – Introduction and Preparation

"No-one can make the fullest use of his/her opportunities,
material or spiritual, in this world without a close and deep study of
his/her nativity."
A. Leo, *Astrology for All*

The desire for greater understanding and awareness of how
human beings fit into the scheme of things within our star (Solar)
system ensures Astrology's survival in the world. Because change
and upheaval continue to disrupt our culture due to natural disasters,
wars, social/political revolution, mental and physical illness, nervous
disorders and accidents, astrology is able to provide us with a strong
base of pattern, rhythm and order that is otherwise, noticeably
missing. One reason behind the existence of this strong base lies in
the essentially constant variety of human nature throughout written
history. Probably, in no previous age, has such a strong base been
more important and so badly needed.

Contrary to public perception modern astrologers are wary of
predicting events. They believe that Astrology's greatest practical
value lies in the diagnosis of a person's character coupled with the
assessment of his/her potential. Having assembled a person's
characteristics we can pick out his/her strengths and weaknesses and
so try to decide what suits him/her best. Armed with the unbiased
insight into his/her qualities of disposition and temperament that
they find themselves endowed with, the belief is that they can then

lead better, happier, more fulfilled and purposeful lives through this enhanced understanding of themselves.

One great difficulty for Astrology is specifying interpretations accurately especially when compared with that of specifying the contents of natal charts. The accuracy of character interpretations, being abstract, is much broader but could become improved with more experience of working with combined natal charts coupled with greater confidence in their correctness.   Hone and Mayo recommended the use of keywords that tended to introduce an astrologer's subjectivity at an early stage and placed significant emphasis on preparation for interpretation.   All this involved considerable time and effort, producing a stilted character assessment that then required converting into acceptable English.

A possible alternative method uses interpretations of indicators published by eminent astrologers based on their long, hard work, built-up experience and special aptitude, together with logical deduction and good practice. Blending these interpretations into an acceptable result also takes time and effort and produces a somewhat stilted result but it has the virtues of being more objective and more impartial. On balance, we shall use this method.

Previously we saw that in all likelihood we derive our character from our genes. We also derive our character from our natal charts. What we have here is two potential descriptions of the same thing. Presently the astrological description of our character is much more readily accessible. The interpretation of natal charts is important for parents because it provides a valuable guide to help them to raise their children. It also becomes important for the children from the start of adulthood onwards.   Traditionally we derived our astrological character by interpreting the indicators present in our birth chart alone but we shall use epoch charts to the same extent as well for this purpose. We base this on the equal, two-strand structure of DNA (see Chapter 1) that became established at our Moment of Fertilisation (or the Pre-Natal Epoch, see Chapters 1 and 4). This justifies our usage of the epoch chart for interpretation purposes but at the moment there seems no real justification for, say, associating the second strand of DNA with the birth chart, apart from that deriving from the validity of the empirical whole of Natal Astrology used up to now. However, examples in 'When Scorpio Ruled the World' seem to show, also empirically, that the combination of interpretations of matched Epoch and Birth charts works well.

There are three main indicators for interpretation for both Epoch and Birth charts; these comprise the positions of the Sun, of the Moon and of the Morin Point. We could use a full-blown set of interpretations of indicators but, more practically, we can create a relevant Person Summary that will cover the most important characteristics of a person that should suffice for our purposes. The indicators that we shall use at both Epoch and Birth for assembling a Person Summary are:

1)   Planet Distribution and Overall Chart Shaping.
2)   Special Interplanetary Aspect Patterns.
3)   Sun and Moon sign combination.
4)   Sun and Moon House combination.
5)   Strongest Aspects to the Sun and Moon only.
6)   Morin Point by sign and Decanate.
7)   Chart Ruler in sign, House and the strongest aspects it receives.
8)   Rising Planets and Retrograde Personal Planets.

We take our Planet Distribution, Overall Chart Shaping and Special Interplanetary Aspect Pattern interpretations from two of Marc Edmund Jones's (1888 – 1980) books: "How to Learn Astrology" and "A Guide to Horoscope Interpretation". M. E. Jones was an American astrologer and author of 4 astrological books. He founded the Sabian Assembly in 1922.

We use interpretations for Sun-Moon Sign combinations from Alan Leo's (1860-1917) "Astrology for All" book and Morin Point Decanate interpretations from his "How to Judge a Nativity" book. Alan Leo was a British astrologer and is regarded as the father of modern Astrology. He wrote thirty books on Astrology and founded "The Astrological Lodge of London" in 1915.

From M. E. Hone (1892-1969) and R. C. Davison (1914-1985), two British astrologers, we abstract interpretations for aspects to the Sun and Moon, and for Ruler and Rising Planets by Sign, by House and by strongest aspects from "The Modern Textbook of Astrology" (MEH) and from "Astrology, How to Cast Your Horoscope" (RCD).

We take Sun-Moon House combination interpretations and aspecting planets House relationships for the Sun, Moon, Ruler and Rising Planets from R. Pelletier's (1927-)"Planets in Houses". He is an American astrologer.

We extract Morin Point Sign interpretations from F. X. King's (1923-1994) "The Cosmic Influence", a British astrologer, and we use Retrograde Personal Planet interpretations by Sign and by House from "Karmic Astrology – Retrogrades and Reincarnation", by M. Schulman, an American astrologer.

All the foregoing books are readily available at a reasonable price through the Internet.

If we should wish to extend this set of indicators to create a full description of combined interpretations then we could also include:

1) Planetary sign synthesis plus quality and element totals.

2) Angular, succedent and cadent planetary totals.

3) Remaining personal planets such as Mercury, Venus and Mars together with their strongest aspects.

4) Positive and negative planet totals.

5) Unaspected planets.

6) Other Retrograde planets.

7) Rulerships, Exaltations and Mutual Receptions.

8) Detriments and Falls.

9) Part of Fortune (Morin Point + Moon – Sun).

10) Dragon's Head (Moon's Node).

11) Parallels of Declination (both conjunction and opposition).

At the very least, we need to be aware of these added indicators when deriving our Person Summaries.

In the spirit of 'pure eyes and Christian hearts' we can complete this part of the book by reminding ourselves that astrologers need to remain professional in order to instil confidence in others and so enhance Astrology's reputation. The qualities they require are good time keeping, thoroughness, accuracy, conservatism and reliability. Additionally they need to be scrupulous in observing confidentiality and in obtaining permission to reproduce any interesting information. They need to resist arrogance, cleverness, sensationalism and the foretelling of inadvisable events such as the time of death, which at no time is certain for anyone. Finally, they need to be helpful and constructive to clients rather than simply factual.

Let us now examine the derivation of 'Heaven's Message' for Diana, Princess of Wales.

- -

CHAPTER 9

Diana Frances Spencer – Princess of Wales

"I'd like to be a Queen of People's Hearts."

First of all let us remind ourselves briefly about Diana:

Diana was a member of the British royal family and an international personality of the late 20th century as the first wife of Charles, Prince of Wales, whom she married in 1981. The marriage produced two sons, Princes William and Harry, currently 2nd and 3rd in line to the English throne.

Diana was born into an old aristocratic English family with royal ancestry. From the announcement of her engagement she remained the focus of worldwide media scrutiny before, during and after her marriage, which ended in divorce in 1996. The media attention continued following her death in a car crash in Paris in 1997 and in the subsequent display of public mourning. Diana received recognition for her charity work and for her support of the International Campaign to Ban Landmines. From 1989 she had been the president of London's Great Ormond Street Hospital for Children.

- -

Figure 1: Epoch Chart and Aspect Grid for Diana, Princess of Wales.

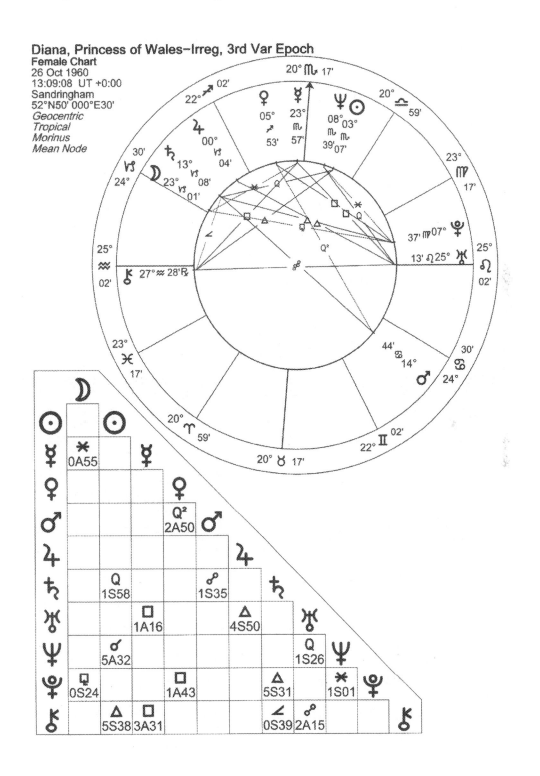

Let us now introduce the main indicators and their interpretations in Diana's Epoch chart:

Diana was born on the 1st July, 1961 at 19:45 at Sandringham, Norfolk, England to John Spencer and Frances Roche, the youngest of three daughters, with one younger brother to follow. Her Epoch (see Figure 1) occurred on the 26th October, 1960 at 13:09. The planetary distribution in the chart is South (above the Morin Point) meaning that she was mainly objective (concerned mainly with practical and visible things). The overall shaping of the chart is a bucket with a singleton, anticlockwise Mars as the handle planet in Cancer in the 6th House. Retrograde Chiron rising in Aquarius, in opposition to the ruler, Uranus, forms the rim of the bucket. This means that Diana would have had a rather uncompromising direction to her life-effort, that she would be strongly emotional and intuitive and that she would have worked hard for the care of others. The opposition of Mars to Saturn indicates that her results would have had to be battled for. There is a fixed T-square with Mercury at the focal point (being bi-square to Chiron and to Uranus) that shows that she became conditioned to trying circumstances but not without nervous strain. Relief of strain (mediation) here could have been provided by activities connected with the Sun, with the Moon and with Jupiter, i.e. charity, commonsense and a vibrant personality. The Sun in Scorpio – Moon in Capricorn polarity shows pride, self-indulgence, perseverance and a rather hard nature, whereas the Sun in the 9th House – Moon in the 12th House polarity indicates a lack of confidence but an ability to care for the helpless. The Morin Point in the 3rd decanate of Aquarius implies a love of freedom and new ideas but a hatred of interference and no particular inclination to marriage! Uranus in Leo in the 7th House and square to Mercury suggests revolutionary tendencies, brusque speech that loses good contact with others and unusual marriage conditions! Retrograde Chiron rising in Aquarius indicates that she gave humane support in an unusual way to some of the most unfortunate members of society but that some difficulty was involved.

Normally we would divide the interpretations presented in the following Tables for Epoch and Birth into four groups, namely: character, relationships, career and health using a different coloured highlighter for each.   Instead, what we have done is to present interpretations belonging to the character group in italics, those for the relationships group in bold type, those for the career group in normal type and those for the small health group as normal type underlined.   We have then subdivided the interpretations for the three main groups into smaller sections, as follows: we split the Character group into 'general', 'mentality' and 'lifestyle' and place G, M or LS in brackets at the end of each piece of character interpretation throughout the Tables to specify which section each piece belongs to. Similarly, we split the Relationships group into four sections, i.e. 'others', 'friends', 'family' and 'lover' and place O, Fr, Fm and L in brackets after each piece of relationships interpretation throughout the Tables to specify which section each piece belongs to. Finally, we split the Career group into 'early', 'middle', 'late' and 'retirement' and place E, Mi, La and R in brackets after each piece of career interpretation throughout the Tables as required. This we have done as shown throughout the Tables.

Fortunately, most of what we have presented in this chapter up to now could be carried out using a computer program.

Indicators and Their Interpretations for Diana's Epoch Chart

Indicator	Interpretation
1) Planet Distribution is S. Overall Chart Shaping: Bucket, Mars in Cancer in 6th House anticlockwise handle, singleton, opposition Saturn. 7th to 12th	*Mainly objective.* (G) An important interest in her life and a rather uncompromising direction to her life-effort. (E) *No desire to preserve herself or to conserve her resources. (LS)* Adapted her allegiances to lines along which she could make her efforts count for the most. (M) *Dipped deeply into life and poured forth the gathered results of her experiences with unremitting zeal. (LS)* **Inspirer but also possible malcontent. (O)** *Strongly emotional and intuitive. (G) The conservative desire to work for the care of others and to collect and maintain family and home would have been coupled with difficult touchiness quickly roused. Energy spent in hard and unstinting work and expects the same from others. (LS)* <u>Strengthened health but liable to feverish complaints.</u> Patient working out of what is begun but not with ease. Results must be battled for. Narrowness engendered produces selfishness and egocentricity. Hardship is endured and sternness results. (Mi) <u>Danger of accidents by scalds, burns and falling. Physical overstrain risked.</u> It bothered her to work without recognition but she had to accept this situation until she was more confident about her abilities. Those who benefited from her services remembered her with gratitude. (E)
2) Special Interplanetary Aspect patterns. Fixed T-Square: Chiron rising opposition Uranus with Mercury (focus) bi-square to both: 4th to 7th and 10th to 1st. (Mediation by	*An inclination to let matters remain as they are and put up with them. Became conditioned to trying circumstances but not without nervous strain. (LS) Penetrative with depth of feeling. (G)* Communication in business, politics and all public life attracted her. (E) HER PARTNER WAS PROBABLY THE SOURCE OF HER INSPIRATION FOR CONTINUALLY PROGRESSING TO HIGHER LEVELS IN HER CAREER. Although she needed this urging she also felt that she was free to exploit her

Jupiter, Sun and Saturn possible.)	potential in her own way. (E) Gaining recognition depended entirely on her forcefulness in asserting herself despite hazards. (E)
3) Sun in Scorpio – Moon in Capricorn polarity.	*Pride and self-indulgence but also a great amount of patience, perseverance and endurance. Rather hard nature, self-will, fixity of opinion and habit. Somewhat combative aggressive and alternating at times between extremes of rashness and caution, liberality and thrift. Ambition and determination making attainment possible. (G) Tendency to materialistic thought. (M)* Suitable for some official position in some public body. (E) Tremendous drama critic. (E) **Easily found at variance with siblings, family and public or separated from the former. (Fm)**
4) Sun in 9th House – Moon in 12th House polarity.	Although she may have been more qualified than others, she always felt that she wasn't, and therefore not ready to take on responsibility. Probably she was over qualified for most responsible positions. She was somewhat afraid of making a fool of herself or of being caught without the necessary credentials. This amounted to a powerful defence mechanism to avoid confronting a challenge. If she had felt unqualified, then she should have got the education or training that she needed. She could do much for those who lack the resources to help themselves, so she could have chosen her career with that in mind. Her heart went out to those who were caught in difficult social situations and she could have accomplished more, even with modest resources, than most people would have thought possible. She might have considered a career serving the public through medicine, law, psychology, vocational guidance, nutrition, self-help programs, social service, correction or institutions for the mentally or physically handicapped. The important thing to remember was to find a way to implement her creative imagination and make a substantial contribution to improving society. (E)
5) Moon sextile Mercury, 3rd to 10th.	*Good commonsense mentality and nervous force. (M)* She spent much time pondering what to do with her life and

Sun weakly conjoint Neptune and weakly quintile Saturn. 12th to 10th.	how to establish herself in a satisfying and worthwhile career. She ought not to have compared her skills with those of other people because that would have intimidated her further. (E) *Tendency to the intangible and a lack of concreteness but controlled and kept practical. Attracted to music, art, dancing, psychism, and to spiritual, mystical and maritime matters. (M)* She shouldn't have imagined that she could achieve recognition without some sacrifices. She may have had to work in obscurity at first but she would have become reasonably secure eventually. (E)
6) Morin Point in 3rd Aquarius decanate. Sub-ruler Venus in Sagittarius in the 10th House. Venus square Pluto. 4th to 7th.	*Independence, originality and even eccentricity (M)* **with a love of freedom and a hatred of interference that may have extended to headstrong disregard for the feelings of others. (O)** *Possibly some intellectual interest and attraction to new and unusual ideas and theories. Refined taste and clear discrimination. Her clairvoyant faculty may have been awakened. (M)* **Her fate was affected by marriage or love affairs, yet she was not inclined towards marriage and would have preferred a celibate life. (L)** **Affection was demonstrative and gay but she did not want to be enchained. Freedom often preferred to marriage tending to be too free with affection and unstable. (L)** *Happy in life in the world (LS)* with ambition to succeed but possible disappointment in these. (E) **Affections and partnerships subject to disclosures, upheavals and new starts but with trouble and unpleasantness. (L)** **She worried about whether she could meet the challenges of competition successfully but she found out a lot about her adversaries without their knowledge. Her partner may have questioned her methods but he couldn't deny her effectiveness. (L)**
7) Ruler Uranus in Leo in the 7th House,	*Tendency to headlong freedom at any price, revolutionary. (G)* **Unusual conditions in marriage or partnership. Changes in circumstances in both likely to be hurtful and**

square Mercury,	**unexpected. Partner's eccentricities were exasperating. (L)** *Strong mental action through revolutionary thought but communicativeness became too brusque and independent so that it lost good contact with others. The addiction to the unusual and unconventional was so strong and so awkwardly expressed that she may have become tiresome. (M)*
10th to 10th;	Working with the public was her key to success and fulfilment but it would have involved many responsibilities. The demands of her career may have limited her freedom but through her accomplishments she would have gained
opposition Chiron,	the public's respect eventually and greater freedom. (E) *Charity and support given unusually but with personal stress. (LS)*
7th to 1st.	**She assumed that most people were freer than she was and she said so openly. This was her way of defending her lack of success in competition, which really resulted from a lack of self-confidence. She felt intimidated by a successful partner. (L)**
Weak trine Jupiter,	Tendency that magnetic determination conduced to results through force of personality and belief in self. (Mi)
9th to 11th.	She needed to be progressive in her thinking and to try not to belittle herself for past failures. If she had looked ahead, then she would have realised that with a little planning she could have achieved her goals but her dream needed to have been a vivid one.*(E) Possibly inspirational ideas.(M)*
8) Chiron rising in Aquarius, opposition Uranus.	Support, help and useful work given humanely and unusually (as a wounded healer) to some of the most unfortunate members of society. (Mi)

Turning our attention now to Diana's Birth chart:

Figure 2: Birth Chart and Aspect Grid for Diana, Princess of Wales

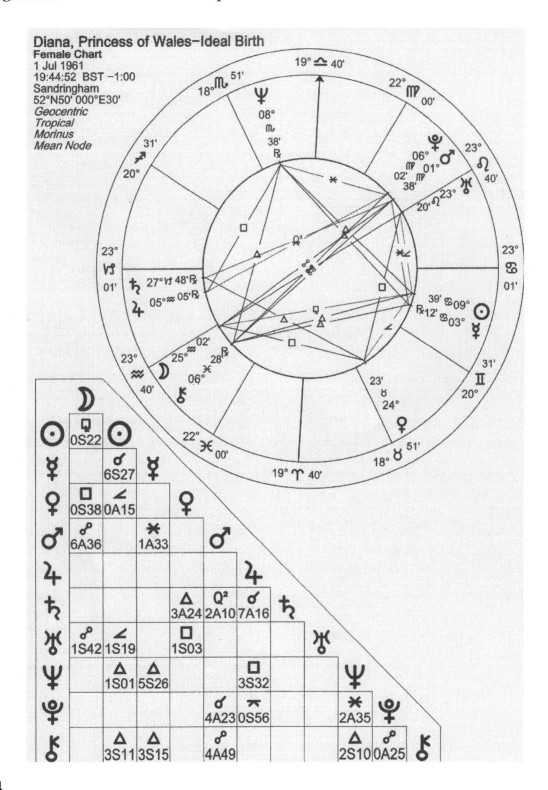

The Epoch generates her Ideal Birth chart (see Figure 2) in which the planets are mainly to the North (below the Morin Point) indicating subjectivity (concerned mainly with spiritual and invisible/abstract things). The chart's overall shaping is Splay with See-Saw tendencies. This suggests an individual personality that deliberates before coming to decisions. There is a Grand trine kite in which Chiron is the focal point in opposition to the Mars-Pluto conjunction and trine both to the Sun-Mercury conjunction as well as to Neptune. All this suggests that she had a well-integrated personality that struggled for harmony in a practical way through support, healing and charity. The fixed T-square with Venus as the focus that is bi-square to the Moon and Uranus, reinforces that one in the Epoch chart, and suggests that her thirst for the good things of life made it difficult for her to hang onto her money. The Sun in Cancer – Moon in Aquarius polarity reveals an inharmonious nature but ability with society/societies and public life, whereas the Sun in the 7th House – Moon in the 2nd House showed that she needed to focus on the affairs of others. The Moon, as part of the fixed T-square, shows an uneasy expression and a lack of harmony at home but that her ideas and intuitions were strong if rather abrasive to others. The Sun trine Neptune reveals a strongly imaginative and idealistic mentality. The Morin Point in the 3rd Capricorn decanate shows a self-controlled personality with practical abilities, shrewd mind and a desire to become a utilitarian. Retrograde Mercury in Cancer in the 6th House suggests that childhood experiences would affect her whole life and make it difficult for her to let go of the past. She would have been better at organising things rather than people but she was a good worker when following established procedures. Retrograde Saturn, the ruler, rising in Capricorn, shows that Diana's feeling of personal inadequacy and of heavy personal responsibilities made it difficult for her to demonstrate how talented she was.

Indicators and Their Interpretation for Diana's Birth Chart

Indicator	Interpretation
1) Planet Distribution N>S; W>E. Overall Planetary Shaping: Splay + See-Saw.	*Somewhat subjective, (G) fate more in the hands of others/circumstances. ((E)* *Individual temperament that resisted pigeon-holing and made for an individual set of purposeful emphases in her life. (G) Individual personality who resisted being limited to any steady point of application. The temperament was inclined to be particular yet impersonal in her interests. Careful hesitation in decision making. (LS)*
2) Special Interplanetary Aspects: Grand Trine Kite in water and earth with square to Jupiter from Neptune. Retrograde Chiron at focal point. Fixed T-square with Venus at focus, bi-square Uranus and the Moon opposite. 4th to 2nd, 10th to 8th.	*Well-integrated personality (G) implying a practical, intense struggle for harmony through support, healing and charity (LS).* *Interpretation for fixed T-square at Epoch reinforced. (LS)* **Suggested happiness and success through love affairs, (L)** prominence (Mi) **and attractive children but also over-possessive of loved ones. (Fm)** *Her desire for the finer things of life made her careless with her financial resources. She found it difficult to hold onto her money when she was tempted to splurge on things she wanted rather than on those she really needed. She needed to be more controlled here. (LS)* Her destiny could have been served by helping to fulfil the needs of the public. Public relations may have been a comfortable field for her benign nature. (E) **She had a talent for meeting people and for making them feel at ease. (O)**
3) Sun in Cancer – Moon in Aquarius polarity.	*Inharmonious nature (G)* but ability with associations and some success in public life. (E) **Tendency to be tactful, careful and diplomatic. (O)** More suitable for external

	activities than for interior life. Ability for painting and general artistic faculties. (E) *She was rather reserved, quiet and self-contained with some inclination for mystical, or psychic, pursuits; she was more sociable and companionable within than she appeared on the surface.* (G) <u>Her eyesight may have needed protection.</u> **One of her parents may have `died early. (Fm)**
4) Sun in 7th House – Moon in 2nd House polarity.	Achieving significance in her life-efforts required focussing on the affairs of others, either personally or professionally. It was necessary for her to concern herself with the public's requirements. Apparently she had every resource she needed to satisfy this kind of responsibility but she may have been apprehensive about the value of applying her efforts this way. Her feelings of insecurity may have caused her to avoid making a commitment because she didn't want to risk losing what she had already gained. She felt that others can help themselves as she had and she resented it when others wanted her always to be available to them. With the right training she might have found that serving people had its own rewards, especially if she had offered professional services. (E)
	Investment counselling, insurance, retirement programs or family counselling were some of the areas in which she could have found ample opportunities to succeed and have the chance to express her talent fully. Her partner needed to have been willing to share the lean years with her until she got established and reached the goals she had defined earlier. Importantly she had had to define them so that she would have been properly motivated to reach them. (E)
5) Moon bi-square Venus and Uranus opposite.

7th to 8th. | ***Uneasy expression of affections and lack of harmony in the home. (Fm)*** *Ideas and intuitions strong through heightened receptivity but likely to be carried out in a perverse or cantankerous manner with nervous tension. (M)* **Frequent breaks with friends. (Fr)**

There was no point in comparing her resources to those of other people unless doing so urged her to succeed in her |

10th to 5th.	endeavours. (Mi) **She was attracted to successful people and she admired them for gaining freedom from economic worries. (O)** She underestimated her abilities and thus failed to capitalise on them. Her fear of risks made it difficult to exploit her creative potential fully. (E) **If she had truly cared about the people she loved, she would have tried to live up to her potential. (Fm)**
Moon sesquiquadrate Sun, 8th to 7th.	**Possible cleavage in her life relating to parents or early childhood. (Fm)** Possible urge to accomplishment. (E) **She was suspicious of people who made demands. (O)** There was no discussion of her financial affairs. (Mi)
6th to 2nd.	She had to meet people on mutually agreeable terms. She took advantage of every opportunity to earn a reasonable income, (Mi) probably by working with people. (E)
Sun bi-semisquare Venus and Uranus;	*Inclination towards beauty and ease but too irresponsibly and carelessly. (G) Tendency to be self-willed, revolutionary, self-important. Disruptive, awkward and brusque. (M)*
3rd to 5th.	**Although she was on good social terms with everyone she met, it was her ability to understand their problems that encouraged them to request her professional skills. Her way with words instantly attracted people's attention. (O)**
12th to 8th.	She underestimated her ability to make an important contribution to society. She was extremely sensitive to human frailty and knew how to solve the problems it causes. (E) **She might have married for financial gain, or simply because she didn't like living alone, which weren't the best reasons. It would have been better to marry because she had met her ideal mate. (L)**
trine Neptune.	*Strong imaginative faculties. Visions, ideals and inspirations but needed strength to actualise them, which she had from Mars handle (see Epoch chart) (M).* <u>She was a good sleeper.</u>
9th to 11th.	As her goals were clearly defined all she needed to realise them was to get the relevant training. She knew that without it her goals were greatly limited. (E)
6) Morin Point in 3rd Capricorn	*A persistent, self-controlled personality capable of achieving*

decanate;	*success through hard work. (G) Practical abilities (G) were combined with a shrewd mind and inner stability. (M)* Circumstances would rule her much more than her ability to make her own destiny. (E) *She desired to be utilitarian and to serve others. (LS)*
Mercury, sub-ruler, retrograde in Cancer	*She kept trying to recreate her childhood, which meant that her upbringing was important for her because her childhood experiences would be carried as a residue all through her life. (LS) Emotionally sensitive she needed independence of thought with emotional security both at the same time. (LS) She tended to grow emotionally possessive of her thoughts, which could have led her into neurotic complexes that she found herself unable to let go of. She had difficulty letting go of the past and moving freely and clearly into the future. She didn't fully understand the idea of growth and kept thinking herself incapable of letting go earlier phases of her life. (M)*
in the 6th House.	*She had a keenly analytical approach to the organisation of her life. (M)* **She attempted to overcome her faults through service to others, which could have been declined at times. Thus there were also frustrations in dealing with people. (O)** She was a good worker at following established procedures and better at organising things than people. (E) *She had a strong tendency to judge herself by her ideals while simultaneously judging others by their actions. (M)*
sextile Mars	*Mind is powerful, courageous and enterprising. (M)* <u>Nervous system strengthened, hence good eyesight, hearing and sense of touch.</u>
11th to 8th.	Her talent allowed her to serve people's needs. Commendably her efforts made their future security possible. She knew that they would happily do favours for her in return, if necessary. (Mi)
Ruler, retrograde Saturn rising in Capricorn,	*There was a feeling of insecurity or inadequacy (M) but this could be a spur to achievement despite obstacles. Likely personal responsibilities could have been heavy. Possible inability to press forward the personal concerns in her life. (LS)* <u>Moods of depression.</u>

	Her self-expression in carefulness, practical ability, patience and success by long and careful planning was likely to come to its best. (Mi) *She tried to restore a previous image of herself. Accustomed to hard work she thrived on the possibility of one day looking back at jobs and projects that she had done well. (LS)* She was capable of locking out interference and directing her life towards a useful purpose enabling her to achieve so much. She worked backwards, i.e. not starting anything until she could visualise the finished product. Her practical approach to life increased. She was especially good at picking up pieces from the past that society had overlooked and making a great life's work out of such seemingly useless fragments, probably because she could not tolerate waste. The amount of inner meaning these achievements brought to her was the most important thing to her. She became ready to bring to fruition much labour along a given path. (Mi)
	She tried to find an impressive and formidable identity structure that the world around her could vibrate to. Something in her was lacking and she had a strong tendency to compensate. (LS) **There were barriers between her and the people she would have liked to get close to. A type of non-trusting attitude was pervasive because she had felt shut out, or closed off, from what she had tried to reach. Instead of facing this she tried to be important so that others would recognise her and perhaps relate to her in a way in which she could not be hurt. (O)** *She was highly sensitive inside despite appearances. (M) She was learning how to stand on her own two feet and this slow process made her fearful that anybody might knock her down before she had built her own foundation. (LS)*
trine Venus,	**Limitation of affection or of a happy social life had its reward in a serious, one-pointed direction. Love may have meant sacrifice or a life lonely except for the chosen one. Partnerships would have been a serious matter but successful in a practical way. (L)**
9th to 5th.	*She was quite talented but she had difficulty showing it. Her*

90

	natural gifts could probably have been developed without extensive formal training, provided that she had learnt to use them efficiently. (G)
8) Uranus, Mars and Pluto in the 8th House (mainly malasp).	<u>Possible sudden, quick and painful death in a public place.</u>

Now we write out all the interpretations again but this time according to their divided groups and sections (see Appendix 1). For example, let's examine Diana's Relationships – Lover section. The phrases and sentences we have written down in order as we met them are:

There was warmth in sexual relations (1a). Her fate was affected by marriage/love affairs, and yet she was not inclined to marriage and may well have preferred a celibate life (3). Affection was demonstrative and gay but did not want to be enchained (1). Freedom was often preferred to marriage as she tended to be too free with affections and unstable (1b). Affections and partnerships were subject to disclosures, upheavals and new starts but with trouble and unpleasantness (1c). She worried about whether she could meet the challenge of competition successfully but she found out a lot about her adversaries without their knowing it (6a). Her partner may have questioned her methods but he couldn't deny her effectiveness (6b). There were unusual conditions in marriage and partnerships (4). Changes in circumstances in both were likely to be hurtful and often unexpected (4a). Her partner's eccentricities caused exasperation (5a). She felt inhibited by a successful partner (5). The assumption of others' greater freedom was her way of defending her lack of success in competition, which really resulted from a lack of self-confidence

(6). She might have married for financial gain or simply because she didn't like living alone, which were not the best reasons (3a). It would have been better to marry because she felt she had met her ideal mate (3b). Limitation of affection, or of a happy social life, had its reward in a serious, one-pointed direction (2). Love may have meant sacrifice or a life lonely except for the chosen one (2a). Partnerships will have been a serious matter but successful in a practical way (2b).'

We have put in numbers and letters at the end of each sentence starting for example, with early relationships, then moving onto partnerships, marriage situation and spouse. The section can now be blended by rewriting it in the order indicated so that it now reads:

'Diana's affections were demonstrative and gay with warmth in sexual relations but she didn't want to be imprisoned in a relationship. She often preferred freedom to marriage, tending to be too free with her affections and unstable. Her affections and partnerships were subject to disclosures, upheavals and new starts creating trouble and unpleasantness. However, limitation of affection, or of a happy social life, had its reward in a narrow, single direction. Love may have meant sacrifice or a life lonely except for the chosen one. Such partnerships would have been a serious matter but successful in a practical way. Her fate was affected by marriage or love affairs, and yet she was not that inclined to marriage and may well have preferred a celibate life. She may have married for financial gain or simply because she didn't like living alone, which were not the best reasons. She would have done better to marry because she felt she had met her ideal mate. Unusual conditions existed in her marriage and partnerships. Changes in circumstances in both were likely to be hurtful and often unexpected. She felt intimidated by a successful partner and his eccentricities caused exasperation. Her assumption of others' greater freedom was her way of defending her lack of success in competition (for her husband), which really resulted from a lack of self-confidence. She worried about whether she could meet the challenge of competition (e.g. Camilla) successfully and she found out a lot about her adversaries without their knowing it. Her husband may have questioned her methods but he couldn't deny her effectiveness.'

Possibly the whole synthesis process is somewhat akin to that a new born baby automatically adopts as he/she tries to make sense of all the signals his/her brain receives from his/her five senses.

Following the process we have, in fact, converted the whole of Diana's interpretation into its four groups and their respective sections (see Appendix 2). Although this seems understandable enough, it should undergo polishing to turn it into 'good/proper' English before submission to a client. This whole, polished interpretation then constitutes Diana's "Heaven's Message". Additionally, for submission-to-a-client purposes, we need a suitable introduction to "Heaven's Message", perhaps along the following lines:

Dear Princess Diana,

Heaven's Message

Most of us know that the Signs of the Zodiac are the well-known part of Astrology. Newspapers and magazines emphasise that Sign containing the Sun since we can all know our own Sign from our individual dates of birth. However, serious astrologers know that the Sign ascending over the Horizon is at least of equal importance. But this ascending Sign can only be found when the moment of birth is known, and is therefore specific for the individual for whom the chart is drawn up. In the way that the Sun is an important planet for men so the Moon is an important planet for women, although both are important for both sexes.

Actually, there are two moments, that of birth and that of fertilisation, that are important astrologically. In all probability we derive our character from our genes that became established at our Moment of Fertilisation (our Epoch). This Epoch time perhaps shows the inherent character of the new individual about to manifest in the flesh, whereas the Birth time denotes the actual personal conditions into which the individual is born. We combine the interpretations from the Epoch and Birth charts to generate "Heaven's Message" for the individual under consideration.

Please find enclosed your Epoch and Birth charts together with several pages of combined interpretation. Please note that none of the interpretation is mine; I have simply taken the interpretations of the various indicators from standard textbooks and have tried to blend them into a readily understandable whole.

Specifically your own Birth chart shows that:

The Sign containing the Morin Point is Capricorn.

The Sign containing the Moon is Aquarius.

The Sign containing the Sun is Cancer.

Similarly, your Epoch chart shows that:

The Sign containing the Morin Point is Aquarius.

The Sign containing the Moon is Capricorn.

The Sign containing the Sun is Scorpio.

Hence your character is mostly a mixture of the traits associated with Capricorn, Aquarius, Cancer and Scorpio.

"The Athenians do not mind a man being clever,

so long as he does not impart his cleverness to others."

Plato, *Euthyphro*

"The ideal should never touch the real."

Schiller, *To Goethe*

"God made thee perfect, not immutable."

Milton, *Paradise Lost*

"Skill and confidence are an unconquered army."

George Herbert, *Jacula Prudentum*

Probably it is best that you yourself should not judge the interpretation but rather let someone who knows you well judge it with you. Basically "Heaven's Message" attempts to supply the requirements for satisfying the old Greek dictum, "Man, know thyself" (presumably both individually and collectively).

The general idea is for you to decide what suits you best, to build on your strengths, to guard against your weaknesses and to reinforce your own personal judgement. In this way your "Heaven's Message" tries to be useful.

- -

We now present her Person Summary in a well-written and readily understandable form from that given in Appendix 4 without altering any of the meaning or its emphasis significantly:

Diana's Person Summary

Character

<u>General:</u> Strongly emotional and intuitive, Diana had a rather hard nature, great self-will, fixity of habit and opinion together with a somewhat combative disposition that alternated between extremes of rashness and caution. On the one hand, she was proud and self-indulgent but on the other possessed patience, perseverance, persistence and self-control that was capable of achieving success through hard work. Practical abilities were combined with a shrewd mind and firm inner stability. Ambition and determination made high attainment possible. However, she also had a rebellious tendency to pursue headlong freedom at any price. She had an individual temperament that robustly resisted pigeon-holing, with a set of purposeful emphases in her life. Although she was a well-integrated personality she had a somewhat inharmonious nature that may have experienced difficulty in making decisions. On first meeting she appeared to be rather reserved, quiet and self-controlled but, despite appearances, she was highly sensitive inside. She also had inclinations towards beauty, art, dancing and music but her approach to them was somewhat careless and cavalier. Her charts further indicate an interest in maritime, mystical and psychic pursuits. Overall she was quite talented but had difficulty showing

it. Probably her natural gifts could have been developed without external, formal training, had she learnt to use them efficiently.

Mentality: Diana   had   a   feeling   of   personal insecurity/inadequacy but this could have proved a spur to achievement despite obstacles.   Mentally she was intense and penetrating, with depth of feeling and a tendency towards materialistic thought. Possibly this lively mentality included some intellectual interests with an attraction for new and unusual ideas. She possessed commonsense and nervous energy. Her forceful, courageous and enterprising qualities made her judge herself by her motives and ideals, while, at the same time, judging others by their actions. She had an analytical approach to the organisation of her life, with refined tastes and clear discrimination.   However, communicating her sometimes unorthodox ideas and strong intuitions could become strident and thus alienate others particularly those close to her. This was noticeably so because her notions and ideas were often unrealistic. On balance, her absorption in her own thoughts and emotions led her into chronic, neurotic complexes that made it difficult for her to let go of the past and move clearly and freely into the future. As a result she didn't fully appreciate the idea of growth and kept thinking herself incapable of letting go of earlier phases of her life.

Lifestyle: Something within her was lacking and she had a strong tendency to compensate. She was learning how to stand on her own two feet but this slow process made her fearful that somebody might knock her down before she had built up her own foundation. She set out to develop an impressive and formidable identity that the world around her could respond to. Most of all she spent her life building a structure of rules that ultimately would provide the building blocks for this identity that she wanted to achieve, which she could well have succeeded in doing.

She kept trying to restore a previous, childhood image of herself. This meant that her upbringing was important to her because her childhood experiences would be carried as a residue all through her life. Emotionally sensitive, she had needed independence of thought as well as emotional security, simultaneously, while she was growing up, which her unstable background and the divorce of her parents denied her.

Initially her temperament inclined her to a life of disinterested service. As an intense personality, who could not be limited to any steady point of application, she desired to be useful to others. She embarked on a practical, intense struggle for widespread harmony through support, healing and charity. Accustomed to hard work she thrived on the possibility of one day looking back at jobs and projects that she had done well. She devoted time and energy to hard and unstinting work and she expected the same from others. She had little desire to preserve herself or to conserve her resources. She dipped deeply into life and poured forth the gathered results of her experiences with unremitting zeal. Her desire to work for others at the same time as maintaining family and home resulted in difficult touchiness, quickly roused. Accordingly, personal responsibilities became a burden to her and restricted her ability to press forward the personal concerns of her life. This may well have led to an inclination to let difficulties remain as they were and put up with them so that she became conditioned to trying circumstances but not without nervous stress. Thus charity, support and help tended to be given by her impulsively and to an unusual degree, which drew people to her, but which could not be accomplished without personal strain.

In addition she may have been greedy for the good things of life and this made her careless with her financial resources. She then found it difficult to hold onto her money when she was tempted to splurge on things she wanted rather than on those she really needed. Probably, in this area, she needed to be more controlled.

Relationships

Her initial approach to meeting people in general was careful, tactful and diplomatic but she was more sociable and companionable within than she appeared on the surface. She was good in public because of her diplomatic, warm manner and her way with words instantly attracted people's attention. Thus she had a talent for meeting people and making them feel at ease. But although she was on good social terms with everyone she met it was her ability to understand their problems that encouraged them to request her professional skills. She inspired others but was herself a malcontent. There was a love of freedom and a hatred of interference that sometimes extended to a headstrong disregard for the feelings of others. She assumed that most people were freer than she was given her position and role in life, and she said so openly. Although she was attracted to successful people, whom she admired for gaining freedom from economic worries, she did not trust them because she felt shut out, or closed off from, what she herself had tried to reach. Hence there were barriers between her and the people she wanted to get close to. Instead of facing this she strove to be important in her own right so that the world would recognise her and others would perhaps relate to her in a way which would not cause her hurt. Therefore she tried to overcome her difficulties through service to others, which brought frustrations as well as successes in her dealing with people.

Friends: Diana experienced frequent breaks with friends.

Family: Her Birth chart indicates the possibility of a cleavage in Diana's life relating to parents, one of whom may have died early. (Her father almost died from a stroke in 1979 when she was 18 and had not been expected to live but did so for a further 12 years) and/or to early childhood (her parents divorced when she was 7). Thus there was a lack of harmony and the normal expression of affection at home. She easily found herself at odds with, or separated from, siblings, family and public. Later on, she had attractive children and could have become overly possessive of loved ones. If she had been able to care truly for the people she loved she may have become able to live up to her potential.

Lover: Diana's affections were demonstrative and there was warmth in sexual relations but she didn't want to be restricted, or tied down. She may have preferred freedom to marriage, tending to be too free with her affections and unstable. Her partnerships and affections were subject to disclosures, upheavals and new starts, repeatedly accompanied by trouble and unpleasantness. However, limitation of affection, or of a happy social life, had its reward in a serious, single direction (her marriage to Prince Charles). Love may have meant sacrifice, or a life lonely except for the chosen one. Such a partnership would have been a serious matter but successful in a practical way. Her fate was affected by marriage or love affairs, and yet she was not that inclined to marriage and may well have preferred a celibate life. She might have married for material gain, or simply because she didn't like living alone, which were not the best reasons. She would have done better to marry because she had met her ideal mate. Unusual conditions existed in her marriage and partnerships. Changes in circumstances in both were likely to be hurtful and unexpected. She felt intimidated by a successful partner and his eccentricities caused exasperation. Her assumption of rivals' greater freedom was her way of defending her lack of success in competition for her husband, which really resulted from a lack of self-confidence. She worried about whether she could successfully meet the challenges of this sort of competition and she found out a lot about her adversaries without their knowing it. Her husband may have questioned her methods but he couldn't deny her effectiveness.

Career

Early: Circumstances would rule Diana much more than her ability to make her own destiny. Her fear of risks made it difficult for her to exploit her creative potential. She underestimated her ability to make an important contribution to society and so failed to capitalise on it. Although she may have been more talented than others she always felt that she wasn't and so was not ready to take on responsibility. She was somewhat afraid of making a fool of herself or of being caught without the necessary credentials (given her poor educational record). This amounted to a powerful defence mechanism to avoid confronting a challenge. In fact she was probably over-talented for the demands of most responsible positions but if she had felt unqualified then she should have got the education or training she needed (e.g. for nursing). Unsuccessful early ambitions could have led to disappointment. She needed to be progressive in her thinking and to endeavour not to belittle herself because of past failures. She should have tried not to compare her skills with those of other people because that would have intimidated her further. However, she mustn't have imagined that she could have achieved recognition without some sacrifices. Gaining recognition depended entirely on her own forcefulness in asserting herself despite hazards. The important thing to remember was to find a way to implement her creative imagination and make a substantial contribution.

She had spent much time pondering what to do with her life and how to establish herself in a satisfying and worthwhile career. If she had looked ahead she would have realised that with a little planning she could have defined and achieved her goals so that she would have been properly motivated but her dream needed to have been a vivid one, particularly considering her position as Princess of Wales.

There would have been a need for an important interest in her life making for a rather uncompromising direction to her life-effort. Her destiny would have been served by helping to fulfil the needs of the public. Indeed public relations might have been a comfortable field for her relatively benign nature. She was a good worker at following past, established procedures and better at organising things than people. She was more suitable for outdoor activities than for a life indoors. Working with the public was the key to her success and fulfilment but it would have involved many responsibilities.

She did much for those who lacked the resources to help themselves and so she could have chosen a career with that in mind. She was extremely sensitive to human frailty and knew how to solve the problems it caused. Her heart went out to those who were caught in difficult social situations and she accomplished much, even with modest resources, than most people would have thought possible.

She had ability for painting, music and dancing with a general artistic aptitude.

Middle: Had Diana not become a member of the Royal Family, she probably would have earned her living by working with people. She would have achieved significance in her life-efforts by focusing on the affairs of others either personally or professionally. Hence it was necessary for her to allow her talents to serve the public's concerns. Fortunately she had every resource she needed to satisfy this kind of responsibility but she may have been apprehensive about the value of applying her efforts in this way. Her feelings of insecurity may have caused her to avoid making a commitment because she didn't want to risk losing what she had already gained (probably becoming such a public celebrity was not commensurate with her marriage to Prince Charles). Her practical ability, care and patience, coupled with long and ambitious planning, had brought success, but results had had to be battled for. The nervousness engendered by this produced selfishness and egocentricity. She was hardened by what she had experienced. She felt that everyone could help themselves as she had done and she resented it when others wanted her always to be available to them. Consequently she wished to meet people on mutually agreeable terms. Thus, because of her heavy responsibilities, she adapted her allegiances to lines along which she could make her efforts count for the most. Diana achieved results through force of personality and belief in her own public role. She was capable of locking out interference and of directing her life towards a useful purpose. She worked backwards, i.e. she never started anything until she could visualise the finished product. Her practical approach to life increased and she would have become ready to bring to fruition everything she had striven for.

Diana was especially good at picking up issues from the past that society had overlooked and making a great life's work out of seemingly broken people (e.g. the victims of landmine explosions), probably because she could not tolerate the waste of human life. Support, help and useful work was given humanely, unusually and impulsively to these most unfortunate members of society. Commendably her efforts made their future security possible. She knew that they would happily do favours for her, on return, if necessary. The amount of inner meaning these sorts of achievements brought to her was the most important thing to her.

Health

Diana had strong health and nervous system; hence good eyesight (despite a possible need for protection), hearing and sense of touch. She was a good sleeper but she risked physical overstrain and was subject to moods of depression. She was liable to feverish complaints, to accidents by burns and scalds and to falls.

Unfortunately there was an indication of a sudden, quick and painful death in a public place – one which was so dramatically realised in 1997 in Paris.

Suggestions Following from Diana's Person Summary

1)   Try to be more aware of your revolutionary tendency so that you can recognise it in its various guises and mitigate it when it arises.

2)   Try to make allowances for yourself as a result of your parents' divorce that denied you the emotional security and the independent thought that you needed simultaneously during your childhood. Try to replace any childhood perceptions of yourself with more realistic and current, adult ones.

3)   Try to make more allowances for others, to be somewhat less possessive of loved ones and to be a little more trusting of those in authority.

4)   Try to be more discriminating regarding your love affairs.

5)   Work on feeling good about yourself.

6)   Your charts strongly suggest that, apart from your family, your charitable work constitutes your personal, most important interest in life.

We can hope that all the content of this chapter could be carried out by means of a computer program. However, at the very least, the tasks of synthesising, blending and the final polishing would need considerable monitoring by the astrologer.

Reference: 'Diana: Her True Story, Commemorative Edition', A. Morton, Simon & Shuster, London, UK, 1997.

- -

CHAPTER 10

President Theodore Roosevelt (TR).

"Speak softly and carry a big stick"

First let us remind ourselves a little about TR:

T. R. Roosevelt was the 26th President of the United States. He is remembered for his energetic persona, his range of interests and achievements, his leadership of the Progressive Movement, his model of masculinity and his "cowboy" image. He was a leader of the Republican Party and founder of the short-lived Bull Moose Party of 1912. Before becoming President (1901-1909) he held offices at the municipal, state and federal level of government. Roosevelt's achievements as a naturalist, explorer, hunter, author and soldier are as much a part of his fame as any office he held as a politician.

Born to a wealthy family, Roosevelt was a sickly child, who stayed at home studying natural history. In response to his physical weakness, he embraced a strenuous life. He attended Harvard, where he boxed and developed an interest in naval affairs. A year out of Harvard he ran for a seat in the state legislature. His first historical book, "The Naval War of 1812", published in 1882, established his reputation as a serious historian. After a few years of living in the Badlands, Roosevelt returned to New York City, where he gained fame for fighting police corruption. He was effectively running the U.S. Department of the Navy when the Spanish-

American War broke out; he resigned and led a small regiment in Cuba known as the Rough Riders, earning himself the Medal of Honour. After the war he returned to New York and was elected governor; two years later he was nominated for, and elected, Vice-President of the United States.

In 1901, President McKinley was assassinated, and Roosevelt became President at the young age of 42. He attempted to move the Republican Party in the direction of progressivism, including trust busting and increased regulation of businesses. Roosevelt coined the phrase "Square Deal" to describe his domestic agenda, emphasising that the average citizen would get a fair share under his policies. As an outdoorsman he promoted the cause of the conservation movement. On the world stage Roosevelt's policies were characterised by his comment "Speak softly and carry a big stick". He was the force behind the completion of the Panama Canal; he sent out the Great White Fleet to display American power, and he negotiated an end to the Russo-Japanese War, for which he won the Nobel Peace Prize.

Roosevelt declined to run for re-election in 1908. After leaving office, he embarked on a safari to Africa and a trip to Europe. On his return to the U.S. a rift developed between Roosevelt and his successor, President Taft. Roosevelt tried to wrest the Republican nomination from Taft, and when he failed, he launched the Bull Moose Party. In the election Roosevelt became the only third party candidate to finish second. After the election he embarked on a major trip to South America; the river on which he travelled now bears his name. He contracted malaria on the trip, which damaged his health, and he died a few years later, aged 60. Roosevelt has been ranked consistently by scholars as one of the greatest U.S. Presidents.

Figure 3: Epoch Chart and Aspect Grid for President T. Roosevelt.

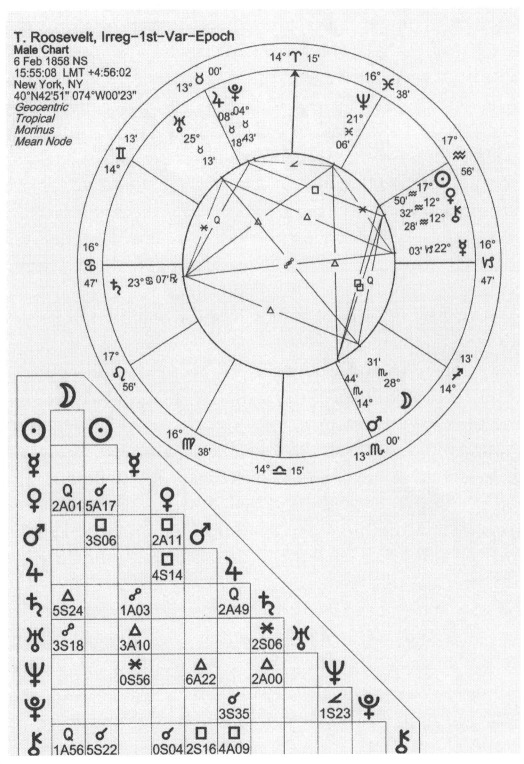

Theodore Roosevelt (TR), the second child and eldest son of Theodore and Mittie was born on the 27th October, 1858 at about 19:45 in New York City, USA (see Figure 4). His Epoch* occurred on the 6th February, 1858 at 15:55 (see Figure 3). The Epoch chart shows that the planets lie mainly to the West suggesting that circumstances and others will decide his destiny. The overall shaping is a bucket with retrograde Saturn rising in Cancer as the somewhat clockwise handle to the rim formed by Uranus opposite to the Moon. The bucket shaping indicates a particular interest in his life and an uncompromising direction to his life-effort. The Saturn handle suggests a feeling of inadequacy that would be a spur to achievement despite difficulties, heavy responsibilities and somewhat impulsive cherishing of loved ones. The Sun in Aquarius – Moon in Scorpio Sign polarity shows a somewhat worldly, selfish, strong-willed and possibly aggressive nature that can play on the nature of others, whereas the Sun in the 8th – Moon in 6th House polarity reveals a requirement to satisfy the needs of others. The Sun square Mars indicates overstrain by overdoing and the Moon opposite to Uranus implies strong ideas and intuitions but which are communicated awkwardly. The Morin Point in the 2nd Cancer decanate shows sensitivity, domestic ties, family interests, impressionable attachments, love of travel and a vital need for friendship. The Moon was his ruling planet (already just mentioned) and retrograde Saturn rising in Cancer suggests unattractive expression and physique but a character with industry, economy and fretful self-indulgence. Notice particularly that Venus is exactly conjoint Chiron in Aquarius in the 8th House, which shows his love of charity, support and help given humanely to the lowest subjects and affairs of the society he lived in.

As we have just done with Diana's Interpretations for her natal charts we have divided TR's into the same four groups. Thus interpretations in italics belong to the Character Group; those in bold type belong to the Relationships Group; those in normal type to the Career Group and those in normal type underlined to the Health Group. The three main groups have been subdivided into three or four sections in just the same way as for Diana by assigning capital letters in brackets to them at the end of each piece of interpretation.

Indicators and Their Interpretations for TR's Epoch Chart

Indicator	Interpretation
1) Planetary Distribution: S and W emphasis. Overall Shaping: Bucket.	*Objective (G).* Destiny supplied by fate, circumstances and others (E). An uncompromising direction to his life-effort (M). He adapted his allegiances to lines along which he could make his efforts count for the most (M). **Instructor/Inspirer of others (O).** *Dipped deeply into life and poured forth the result of his gathered experiences with unremitting zeal (LS). No basic desire to preserve himself or to conserve his resources (LS).*
Retrograde Saturn rising in Cancer, somewhat clockwise handle.	<u>Rather short stature; nothing pleasing in expression or form of body.</u> *Inclined to fretful self-indulgence (G). Humble, patient (G), remorseful, jealous, peevish (M), discontented, unhappy (G). Industry, thrift, perseverance and economy (G). Contemplative, thoughtful and deeply religious (M).* **Quiet devotion that is unassuming (L/P) and considerate (O).** *Business interests sacrificed for home ones (LS). Public interest sacrificed for private gain (LS). A feeling of personal inadequacy or insecurity (G).* This could prove an impulsive spur to achievement despite obstacles (E). *He could see to the bottom of problems (LS). Personal responsibilities heavy (LS).* <u>Possible moods of depression.</u> **The desire for security and the realisation of a need for caution resulted in a strong feeling for guarding and cherishing that which was under his care (Fam).**
Saturn	Although constructive in a narrow, one-track way order

opposition Mercury	would become dreary planning (M). Mental loneliness resulted because of fear and apprehension (M). Resulting lack of poise forced brusque speech and writing (M).
7th to 7th.	**He was stimulated to match the good judgement he observed in others (O).** It was important to become more self-disciplined in developing his talents to improve his competitive position (E).
Saturn trine Neptune.	His ideals and imaginative intuitions were kept in bounds and given shape and form to make them useful practically (E). *Limitations through maze-like worries cleared up in the long run through patient endurance and quiet keeping out of the limelight (M).*
5th to 9th.	Learning came easily to him and he rarely forgot what he had learned (E). He valued education as the first essential step towards achievement (E). He knew it was the only way to exploit his creativity wisely (E).
Saturn sextile Uranus.	Practical planning and determined self-will united to produce brilliance in management, in science and in unusual ways (E).
3rd to 11th.	**Selective about making friends (Fr). He was drawn to persons who were mature enough to be independent (e.g. Cabot Lodge) (Fr).** He knew that his future financial security must come from using his own resources effectively (M).
Saturn retrograde in Cancer.	*He dwelt on emotions which burdened his early years (LS). He had a high need for security (LS).* **His need for protection and safety was transferred to his father (Fam). When he did try to come out of himself he was not sure that he would have been fully accepted by others (O).** *He tended to stifle his emotions as if to save them for the one individual he might have met in the future who would have been symbolic of the past security he had lost (LS). When travelling he would keep identifying each new place with a past he was already comfortable in (LS). In this way he could move through life with a feeling that he was securely rooted, no matter where he was, or with whom, (LS). Because he experienced living in a changing world it would have been better if, instead of trying to make his present life fit into his past, he realised and accepted it within the past security he had known so that he no*

Retrograde Saturn rising.	*longer had to seek it continually in the outer world (LS).* *He tried to find an impressive and formidable identity structure that the world around him could vibrate to (LS). Something within him was lacking and he had a strong tendency to compensate (LS). There were barriers between him and the people he would have liked to get close to (LS). A type of non-trusting attitude was pervasive because he had felt shut out, or closed off, from what he had tried to reach (LS). Instead of facing this problem he tried to be important so that others would recognise him, and perhaps relate to him in a way in which he could not be hurt (LS). Highly sensitive inside, despite external appearances, he was learning how to stand on his own two feet and this slow process made him fearful that anybody could knock him down before he had built his own foundations (LS).*
2) Special Interplanetary Aspect Patterns: Broad fixed T-square. Venus is the focal planet: exactly conjoint Chiron, square Mars and square Jupiter, Weakly mediated by Neptune trine Mars.	*Inclined to let matters remain as they are and so put up with them. He became patiently conditioned to trying circumstances but not without some nervous strain (LS).* **A love of support, help and charity given humanely to the contemporary lowest priorities of society (O). He had a compelling need to become involved with persons who shared his strong desire for warm, sociable relationships (Fr). He was usually on his best behaviour, which he considered a good investment to win someone who attracted him (L/P). He had an ability for dealing with people and a talent for helping them to achieve greater harmony and face the future with greater optimism (O). He was concerned about his partner's needs and pleasures but there may have been some anxiety about his ability to indulge her, or other family members, satisfactorily (Fam).**
3) Sun – Moon Sign Polarity: Sun in Aquarius – Moon in Scorpio.	*Somewhat worldly and selfish nature (G).* **Great ability for playing on the nature of others (O).** *Too positive, self-reliant, self-assertive and proud (G). Very strong willed, not easily influenced or turned aside (G). Irritability, abruptness or aggressiveness possible (G).* **There may have been sorrow through either of his parents (Fam).** His nature could have been useful in the world as he was practical, managerial, businesslike, firm, steady and hard-working (E). Thus he was

	suitable for positions of prominence and responsibility (E). Likely to gain money, property, power or dignity (M).
4) Sun – Moon House Polarity: Sun in 8th House – Moon in 5th House.	Deriving the most benefit from his fine creativity depended on his willingness to satisfy the needs of others (M). His early conditioning may have taught him that he didn't have to get involved with others, or extend a helping hand, if he didn't want to (E). With this attitude, the road to success in his career and relationships would have been paved with frustration and conflict (E). However, with his creativity, he could have made a valuable contribution to society, and he must have had to accept responsibility for making it available (E). A vast world of opportunity opened up when he became aware of this (E).
	Because a comfortable lifestyle was important to him, the best way to get what he wanted and improve the quality of life for others was through a career that involved public service (M). The difference between success and failure was the ability to integrate his feelings with his will so that emotional distress did not interfere with his ability to perform well in his career (M). **Once he relaxed his defence mechanisms and realised that everyone has failings he increased the chance of having satisfactory relationships (L/P). Usually a permanent relationship was the best way for two people in love to fulfil their need for each other, and that didn't mean that one was using the other except in mutual interest (L/P).**
5a) Sun square Mars. 4th to 5th. 5b) Moon opposite Uranus.	<u>Though much may have been achieved, his tendency was to overstrain through overdoing thereby impairing his vitality.</u> *Pugnacious and bad-tempered (G).* <u>Liable to minor accidents.</u> His desire to exploit his creativity may have been frustrated in the beginning but eventually he would have found the freedom when he had learnt to be fully responsible for his actions (E). *His ideas and intuitions were strong through heightened receptivity but might have been carried out in a perverse or cantankerous manner with nervous tension (M).* **Frequent breaks with friends (Fr).**

7th to 11th.	He might have been intimidated by the success of his close friends but this should have aroused him to accept the challenge and try to match them (Fr).
6) Morin Point in Cancer, 2nd decanate. Pluto (decanate ruler) in Taurus in 11th	*Imaginative, fanciful, economical, receptive and tenacious disposition (M).* Fate depends on environment and general surroundings (E). **Domestic ties, family interests (Fam) and impressionable attachments (L/P).** *Psychic and mystical tendencies awakened but also control over the sensations (M). Determination, love of power and travel, ambition but at the expense of some internal receptivity (M).* Fate influenced by conventional notions, acquisitiveness and pride (E). *Utilitarian outlook (M), endurance (G), pensiveness and ability to 'merge' ideas stimulated (M).* **Vital need for friendship and ability to influence friends (Fr).**
7) Ruler, Moon.	See 3), 4) and 5) earlier.
8) Retrograde Saturn rising in Cancer.	See 1) earlier.

Turning our attention now to his Birth chart:

<u>Figure 4:</u> Birth Chart and Aspect Grid for President T. Roosevelt.

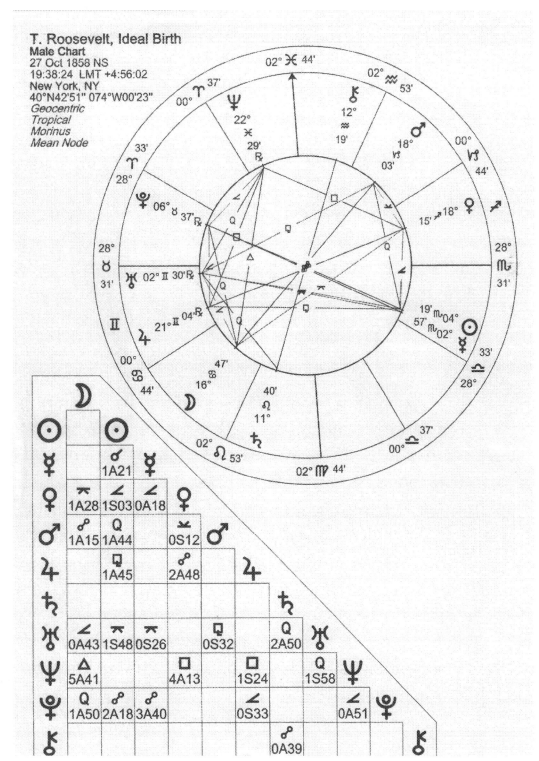

The Epoch generates the Ideal Birth chart as given (see Figure 4). There are seven quintile aspects altogether in both charts, signifying intelligence. For the Birth chart there is a slight preference for an East distribution of the planets, showing that his destiny was partly in his own hands, mainly through a general interest in everything, drive and careful consideration deriving from the Splash-Locomotive-See-Saw shaping of the chart. There is a sesquiquadrate kite with the Sun-Mercury conjunction in Scorpio as the main focus in the 6th House, opposite Pluto. Thus his secretive, penetrative and passionate nature is emphasised as well as personal advancement through ruthless behaviour towards others. The Sun in Scorpio – Moon in Cancer Sign polarity provides harmony and a liking for a man's world but also signifies a propensity for mistakes made as a result of his feelings. The Sun in the 6th House – Moon in the 2nd House polarity shows willingness to develop his basic resources, good judgement and a need to unwind at times. The Moon opposite to Mars reveals a quarrelsome and moody nature and a lack of peace at home. The Morin Point in the 3rd Taurus decanate indicates a tendency to run in a groove, receptivity to parental training and a liking for good food. Venus (ruler) in Sagittarius in the 8th House opposite to Jupiter and square to focal Neptune shows an instability with affections, an overdone, easy charm and a wish to be seen as valuable to society. There was also a tendency to adjust to difficulties regarding friendship and to by-pass them but not always satisfactorily. Retrograde Uranus rising in Gemini suggests a highly active, impatient, frank and curious mentality, an exciting array of friends and a strong tendency to function largely on nervous energy. Asthma, heart, and diarrhoea problems probably all stem from the Sun-Mercury conjunction in Scorpio in the 6th House, as the focal point of the sesquiquadrate kite with its opposition to Pluto. Heart troubles would have been exacerbated by Mars square the Sun in Aquarius at Epoch and bronchial troubles could well have come from Uranus rising in Gemini closely sesquiquadrate to Mars at birth as well as the Moon in the 6th House in Scorpio opposite to Uranus in Taurus at Epoch.

Indicators and Their Interpretations for TR's Birth Chart

Indicator	Interpretation
1) 7 Quintiles in both charts; 4 oppositions in birth chart (only Neptune and Uranus not included); weak trine between Moon and Neptune only favourable aspect. Planetary Distribution (slight E preponderance) and Overall Shaping: Splash-Locomotive-Seesaw	*Intelligence (M). At best a capacity for genuine universal width of interest, drive and careful consideration (M).* Destiny somewhat in his own hands (E).
2) Special Interplanetary Aspect Patterns. Mutable T-square: Neptune, bi-square the Venus and Jupiter benefics, is the focus, 4th to 8th.	*He attempted to adjust to difficulties and to by-pass them but rarely without nervous tension (LS).* *Spiritual and over-inspirational ideas could be brought to fruition within his controlled and moral character (M). His 'hunches' usually would have been right (M).* He had to learn to make appropriate investments to ensure security later in life (M). **Tendency to find it difficult to be free of obligations to people around him in his personal and professional life (O).** He had to discipline himself to make the most of his

117

10th to 2nd. Sesquiquadrate kite. Sun/Mercury conjunction is the focus in Scorpio in the 6th House, opposition Pluto. 1st to 6th. 7th to 12th.	resources because being solvent dispelled his anxieties about the future (M). *He hoped that the public realised how valuable he was to society (LS).* *Well-integrated, but strained personality (M).* *Secretive, penetrative, passionate traits emphasised (M).* **He had a tendency to advance himself through ruthless behaviour towards others (O).** His success in striving for significance depended on how well he used his creativity (E). Self-development was the key (E). He could have become a credit to himself by building a sound mind in a sound body (E). He had to find a way to make a meaningful contribution to society, either through personal or group activities (M). His talent for improving existing social conditions was much needed (M). He was ready to work behind the scenes if necessary (M).
3) Sun – Moon Polarity: Sun in Scorpio and Moon in Cancer.	*Harmonious character that was drawn into mistakes through his feelings and sensations (G).* **He could have been easily led by others into acts of folly (O). An early marriage was recommended because his life might have been influenced for good as his powers of attachment were very strong (L/P).** *He had a hard and practical nature that necessitated his involvement with the world and mixing with men (LS)*, **but he had a kinder and softer side in social matters or in family life (Fam)**. Considerable business ability that earned or inherited money or property, with economic management (M). *Possible psychic or occult tendencies (M).* <u>Good health both from nutrition and digestion. The size of his body was increased resulting in stoutness.</u>
4) Sun – Moon Polarity: Sun in 6th House – Moon in 2nd House.	Because he was so willing to apply himself in developing his resources, he would have derived the greatest possible gains from his efforts (M). He had a talent for increasing the value of his assets (M). His value judgement was well-developed so that he wasted little time and effort in non-productive enterprises (M). His ability to succeed probably

	came from his parents, who taught him to assert himself within the framework of reasonable discipline and responsibility (E). They supported him in his struggle to make his own way (E). He was generally willing to change old habits for better ones so he was rarely locked into an attitude that might have interfered with his continuing progress (M). His inner and outer worlds were sufficiently integrated so that his ambition didn't run into any serious conflicts with his temperament (M). Because of that, success would have been easier to achieve, and he should have gained it fairly early in life (M). **He may have had some problems in relationships; he may have attracted a partner who expected a lot from him so that he really had to extend himself to satisfy these expectations (L/P). His children were the real catalysts in his life, stimulating him to higher levels of performance in providing for them (Fam).** *He had to reserve enough time for himself so that he could unwind and enjoy some of the benefits that he had deserved (LS).*
5a) Sun conjoint Mercury, opposition Pluto 5b) Moon opposite Mars; 6th to 9th. 2nd to 1st.	See 2) earlier. *Moody or quarrelsome nature (G).* **Lack of peace at home (Fam).** Having a high regard for education, he strove constantly to increase his knowledge (M). He knew he could improve his earning ability by being well-informed, so he was willing to invest in getting an education (E). **Fearing the loss of his resources, he asserted himself cautiously towards others (O). He preferred not to be involved in other people's affairs, so he avoided any group functions that required donations of time or money (O).**
6) Morin Point in the 3rd Taurus decanate.	*Some ambition but with an inclination to running in a groove, or becoming too conventional (M), this tended to an over-cautious approach but his intellect and reason were stimulated thereby lessening his intuitive nature (M). His fate depended on his*

.	early environment because there was less power to break away from early training and parental influence (E). His fortune was affected by his innate self-control and his organising power (E). His chastity (once settled and devoted) was also a key to his success (M). *He liked good food (G).*
7) Ruler Venus in 8th, in Sagittarius, opposite Jupiter; 7th to 2nd. semisquare Mercury, 3rd to 6th; semisextile Mars, 12th to 9th. Subruler Saturn in Leo in the 3rd House, opposition Chiron.	*Spiritual pleasures were a joy and happiness (M).* **Too free with affection and unstable but harmonious conditions in sexual relationships (L/P). Gain through partner's money (L/P)** or inherited money or possessions (M). *However, all these desirable happenings didn't always occur without trouble.* **Easy charm intensified but overdone (O). Too many love affairs (L/P),** *love of the easy, the beautiful and the pleasant, at any price (LS).* **Desire for partnership overdone (L/P). Lack of ability to be happy alone (L/P). He wanted so much to measure up to other people's expectations that he tended to overestimate their material advantages as well as their human traits (O). Then he became intimidated because he wanted the same things for himself (O).** **He understood that everyone has weaknesses or flaws which he could overlook when their positive traits were outstanding (O). Generally he was willing to help others with their problems (O).** **Tendency towards a cutting harshness in relationships and intense sexual relations but with quarrels (L/P). Feelings tended to be strong but caused and received hurt (L/P).** **He may have been motivated by a strong spiritual commitment to serve others, in which case his results were much greater than the sacrifices he had made for them (O).** *Wise control, caution and commonsense in all correspondence, communication or literary work (M). Formal education scanty (M). Lack of power to express himself in creative, happy ways (LS). Enjoyment of life did not come easily (LS).*

7th to 9th.	As painful as it seems he absolutely must have had to get some formal education or his future would have seemed limited indeed (E). He needed to define what he hoped to gain in life and to determine the best way to succeed (E). He should have realised that getting an education was a good start (E).
8) Retrograde Uranus rising in Gemini.	<u>Tall stature, light hair and eyes, quick and active in all his movements.</u> *Curious, foreseeing, reforming, progressive and eccentric disposition, passionately fond of science (M). Highly active mental life (M). He tried to find the identity that made him the most comfortable (M). As he was nervous and erratic he was highly influenced by all the available external thought in the world (M). This made it difficult for him to stick to any one topic, or project, for any length of time (M). His interest in exploring all mental possibilities made life a mishmash of scattered ideas and attitudes (M). Without enough confidence in his own uniqueness of thought he tended to identify with the originality of others (M). There was a distinct danger that he could actually lose his grip on reality perspective but he did have control and idealism here to keep his feet on the ground (M). Otherwise he could easily have been diverted away from any realistic goal-oriented approach to life (M). Unconsciously he was highly gullible and so needed to avoid hypnosis or other deep-mind techniques which would have tended to take him too quickly into levels of his being that he would not have been ready to handle (M).* *In fact he was so mentally activated that even his strong interest in sexuality took on more of mind exploration than it did any physical or emotional fulfilment (M). As one with a highly inquiring mind he was the investigator who could not decide on any given chosen path as being the right one for him (M). He tried very many different things but never really settled on any one of them (M). Consequently he knew people from many different walks of life, each one coming from something that he himself would have liked to try (M). One day he may have come to realise that the mental gymnastics he had been using for*

	decades had basically been keeping him from experiencing himself (M).
	He had little interest in the rules and traditions of the society he lived in (LS). He identified with all that was new and unique and rebelled against being caged or pigeon-holed (LS). He strove to establish his own uniqueness so that he could distinguish his own identity from the myriad of identities he saw around him (LS). He tried to express himself as quickly and as spontaneously as he could all the time (M). **This was a poor situation for marriage due to his unpredictability and attempts to break away from the conventional (L/P).** *Change was continuous until he understood that his true purpose was not to dedicate his life to any principle or course of action because that would have smothered his spirit of adventure (LS). Consequently he continued to explore worlds that were wider and with more possibilities than anything he had experienced before (LS). As a first-class seeker he sacrificed much of the comforts of traditional society so that he could be free to discover that which existed just beyond the limits of his contemporaries (LS).*
Quintile 3, 11.	
	He had an exciting array of friends, ranging from the genteel to the coarse (Fr). *He had a unique ability to remain relatively unaffected by the lifestyle of those around him (LS). His cool detachment may have caused him some anxiety later on because he didn't plan ahead, assuming that everything would turn out well (LS).* **With his abundance of ideas he could have done much to shape his future (E). With a little foresight, his financial security and independence were assured (E).**
8th to 6th.	
5th to 9th.	<u>He should have avoided acting hastily or on impulse otherwise he ran the risk of physical exhaustion.</u> *He tended to function largely on nervous energy and he wanted to do everything right away, because he never knew what would happen tomorrow (LS).* **He enjoyed people who weren't afraid to speak their minds, provided they had something worthwhile to say**

12th to 2nd.	**(O).** *His keen perception told him what was right or wrong with the politics of his time, so he could well have become involved in this area (LS).* He alternated between being preoccupied with money and considering it a cross to bear (M). Because of that attitude he may have been on the fringes of poverty (M).
9) Sun/Mercury conjunction strongly afflicted in Scorpio in the 6th House + Uranus rising in Gemini afflicted by the Sun, Mercury and also Mars at birth. Mars square Sun in Aquarius as well as Uranus opposite the Moon at epoch.	<u>Asthma and Diarrhoea (Sun opposition Pluto) caused primarily by the afflicted nature of the Sun at birth. His bronchitis possibly stems from Taurus and afflicted Uranus rising and the Sun's situation at birth as well as by the Moon in Scorpio opposite Uranus in Taurus at Epoch.</u> <u>His heart condition could have derived from Mars square the Sun at Epoch and possibly from the Sun's situation at birth.</u> See "The Encyclopaedia of Medical Astrology", H. L. Cornell, S. Weiser, York Beach, Maine, USA, 1933.

Once again we write the Interpretations out again but this time according to their groups and sections. Appendix 3 presents the whole of TR's interpretations according to their groups and their sections. Each individual section has been reorganised to make it more readily understandable as in Appendix 4 and the resulting whole then needs converting into good English.

As before, by way of illustration, let us examine the 'Relationships Group – Others' section. We have written out the interpretations belonging to this Section as we encountered them as follows:

<u>Others:</u> He was able to deal with people (1). He had a talent for helping people achieve greater harmony and face the future with greater optimism (1d). When he tried to come out of himself he was

not sure that that he would be fully accepted by others (2). He was stimulated to match the good judgement he observed in others (2d). He had great ability in playing on the nature of others (3c). He found it difficult to be free of obligations to people around him in his personal and professional affairs (3a). He could have been led easily into acts of folly by others (3). He had a tendency to advance himself through ruthless behaviour towards others (3d). Fearing the loss of his resources, he asserted himself cautiously towards others (2a). He preferred not to be involved in the affairs of other people so he avoided any group functions that required donations of his time and money (3b). He wanted so much to measure up to other people's expectations that he tended to overestimate their material advantages as well as their human traits (2b). Then he became intimidated because he wanted the same things for himself (2c). He understood that everyone has weaknesses or flaws, which he could overlook when their positive traits were outstanding (2e). Generally he was willing to help others with their problems (1a). He may have been motivated by a strong spiritual commitment to serve others, in which case his results were much greater than the sacrifices he had made for them (1c). He enjoyed people who weren't afraid to speak their minds, provided they had something worthwhile to say (2f). There was a love of support, help and charity given humanely to what, in his era, were the contemporary lowest priorities of society (1b).

We have put in numbers and letters at the end of each sentence starting for example, with more general statements, then moving onto more specific ones. The section can then be blended by rewriting it in the order indicated so that it now reads:

<u>Others</u>: TR was able to deal with people and generally he was willing to help others with their problems. There was a love of support, help and charity given humanely to what, in his era, were the contemporary lowest priorities of society. He may have been motivated by a strong spiritual commitment to serve others, in which case his results were much greater than the sacrifices he had made to gain them. In fact he had a talent for helping people achieve greater harmony and face the future with greater optimism.

When he tried to come out of himself he was not sure that he would be accepted by others. Fearing the loss of his resources he asserted himself cautiously towards others. He wanted so much to measure up to other people's expectations that he tended to overestimate their material advantages as well as their human traits. Then he became intimidated because he wanted the same things for himself. Additionally he was stimulated to match the good judgement he observed in others. He understood that everyone has weaknesses or flaws, which he could overlook when their positive traits were outstanding. For example, he enjoyed people who weren't afraid to speak their minds, provided they had something worthwhile to say. He himself could easily have been led into acts of folly by others. Perhaps as a result, he found it difficult to be free of obligations to people around him in his personal and professional affairs. Accordingly, he preferred not to be involved in the affairs of other people and avoided any group functions that required donations of his time and money. On the other hand, he had a great ability for playing on the nature of others with a tendency to advance himself through ruthless behaviour towards them.

The introduction to TR's polished interpretation will be very similar to Diana's except that in TR's case we can say:

Specifically your own Birth Chart shows that:

The Sign containing the Morin Point is Taurus.

The Sign containing the Sun is Scorpio.

The Sign containing the Moon is Cancer.

And similarly your Epoch Chart shows that:

The Sign containing the Morin Point is Cancer.

The Sign containing the Sun is Aquarius.

The Sign containing the Moon is Scorpio.

Hence you are largely a mixture of the traits associated with Scorpio, Cancer, Taurus and Aquarius.

"Skill and confidence are an unconquered army."

George Herbert, *Jacula Prudentum*

"God made thee perfect not immutable."

Milton, *Paradise Lost*

"Let us make hay while the Sun shines."

Cervantes, *Don Quixote*

"The ideal should never touch the real."

Schiller, *To Goethe*

Probably it is best that you yourself should not judge the interpretation but rather let someone who knows you well judge it with you. Basically "Heaven's Message" attempts to supply the requirements for satisfying the old Greek dictum, "Man, know thyself" (presumably both individually and collectively).

The general idea is for <u>you</u> to decide what suits <u>you</u> best, to build on <u>your</u> strengths, to guard against <u>your</u> weaknesses and to reinforce your own personal judgement. In this way your "Heaven's Message" tries to be useful.

We now present TR's Person Summary as the polished form of Appendix 4 written so that the meanings and their emphases are not altered significantly. Relevant biographical extracts have been included in brackets.

TR's Person Summary

Character

General: There appear to be two sides to TR's character. Firstly, he had a hard, practical and objective nature that necessitated his involvement with the world and mixing with men but he also had an inclination to live in a cocoon, cut off from others. His well-integrated but somewhat worldly, ambitious and selfish nature was too positive, self-reliant, self-assertive and proud. His very strong, enduring will was not easily influenced or turned aside but when thwarted he could become irritated, abrupt, moody, quarrelsome, bad-tempered and pugnacious. As a result his otherwise stable personality was drawn to mistakes through his emotional responses.

On the other hand, and at the same time, he had a feeling of personal insecurity/inadequacy that produced, on the negative side, discontent, unhappiness, excessive thrift and narrow conventionality, while, on the positive side, humility and circumspection. The conflict between these two sides inclined him to fretful, peevish self-indulgence possibly then followed by remorse. He had a love of comfort, good food, travel, the beautiful and the pleasant but, as we have seen, a tougher note was provided by other parts of his nature.

Mentality: TR had determination, love of power and ambition but at the expense of sensitivity to others. Despite his scanty formal education there is no doubt that TR was intelligent. His ideas and intuitions were strong thanks to a highly receptive nature but they were often carried out in a perverse or cantankerous manner, as a result of the nervous tension within his personality. He was so highly active mentally that he tried to express himself as quickly and as spontaneously as possible all the time. Even his strong sexuality remained largely indulged on an intellectual or spiritual level rather than in any physical or emotional fulfilment. An intensely curious and thoughtful individual, he was an investigator who, ironically, could not decide upon any chosen path that would be the right one for himself. He tried many different careers but never really settled on any one of them. Consequently he knew many different people from many walks of life, each one representing an area that he himself would have liked to try. He vainly sought the single identity with which he could feel comfortable. He strove to establish his own uniqueness so that he could distinguish his own identity from the myriad of identities he met around him. He had little interest in the rules and traditions of the society he lived in and identified with all that was new and different, rebelling against being caged or pigeon-holed. As he was nervous and erratic, he was highly influenced by all kinds of current ideas and philosophies. His interest in exploring all mental possibilities tended to make his mind a whirlpool of scattered, unrelated ideas and attitudes. This made it difficult for him to stick to any one topic, or project, for any length of time. As a result he lacked confidence in the uniqueness of his own thoughts and tended to identify with the originality of others. He was therefore in danger of losing his grip on reality but, to counteract that tendency, he did have the self-control and the idealism needed to keep his feet on the ground. Otherwise he could easily have become diverted from any specific aim in life. Unconsciously he was highly gullible and so needed to avoid hypnosis or other deep mind techniques which would have tended to take him too quickly into levels of his being that he would not have been able to handle.

Change was continuous for him until he understood that his true purpose was not to dedicate his life to any one principle or course of action because that would have smothered his spirit of adventure. As a restless seeker after new ideas and experiences he sacrificed much of the comforts of traditional society so that he could be free to discover that which existed just beyond the limits of his contemporaries. Thus he continued to explore areas that were wider and contained more possibilities than anything he had explored before. Eventually he might have come to realise that all these mental gymnastics, indulged in across so many decades, had been keeping him from knowing and coming to terms with himself.

Despite all the negative consequences, his practical outlook and his ability to think and to merge ideas were stimulated. He became able to see to the bottom of problems. He exercised wisdom, caution and commonsense in all correspondence, communication, education or literary work. Although sometimes distracted by anxieties of all kinds, he was able to overcome them in the long run through patient endurance and quiet keeping out of the limelight.

Spiritual and religious pleasures brought him joy and happiness but were not always satisfied easily. There was a secretive, passionate and penetrative side to his nature as well as psychic, occult and mystical tendencies but he was also able to keep these carefully under control.

Lifestyle: TR tended to function largely on nervous energy and he wanted to do everything right away because he never knew what would happen tomorrow. He dipped deeply into life and poured forth the result of his gathered experiences with unremitting zeal. He had no desire to preserve himself or to conserve his resources. His keen perception told him what was right or wrong with contemporary politics, so he was well-equipped to become involved in this area. He had a unique ability to remain relatively unaffected by the behaviour and attitudes of those around him. His cool detachment may have caused him some anxiety later on because he didn't plan ahead, assuming that everything would turn out well. He also appears to have lacked the power to express himself in creative, happy ways, so that despite himself, his enjoyment of life did not come easily. Personal responsibilities were heavy. As a result he attempted to put up with, to adjust to, or to by-pass difficulties, thereby becoming conditioned to trying circumstances but rarely without nervous strain. He dwelt on emotions which had burdened him in his early years during which he had had a high need for security. He tended to repress his emotions as if to save them for the one individual he might meet in the future who would represent and give to him the past security now lost (probably his second wife, Edith). When travelling he would identify each new place with something or somewhere in his past that he was already comfortable with. In this way he could move through life with the feeling that he was securely rooted, no matter where, or with whom, he was. Because he was living in a changing world it would have been better if, instead of trying to make his present life fit into his past, he had allowed the feeling of security enjoyed in the past naturally to impinge on and inform the present, so that he no longer had to seek continually for reassurance.

Something within him was lacking and he tried hard to compensate. There were barriers between him and the people he would have liked to get close to. He did not trust them because he felt shut out, or closed off from, what he wanted to reach. Instead of facing this problem he strove to be important in his own right, so the world would recognise him and others would relate to him in a way that would not cause him hurt. Despite external appearances he was highly sensitive inside. He gradually learnt how to stand on his own two feet but such a slow process made him fearful that anybody might knock him down before he had built a secure foundation. Somehow he had to reserve enough time for himself so that he could unwind and enjoy some of the benefits that he had deserved. In fact a part of him had a love of ease and inactivity but he needed to be careful that business or public interests weren't sacrificed either to home cares or to personal gain.

Relationships

Despite his insecurities, TR was able to deal with people in general, i.e. those with whom he was not in any way intimately involved. He was willing to help others with their problems. He gave humane support, help and charity to those in contemporary society who were considered to be of low priority, e.g. to poor blacks and to oppressed, capitalist labour. He may have been motivated by a strong spiritual commitment to serve others, in which case his results were much greater than the sacrifices he had made to get them. In fact he had a talent for helping people to achieve greater harmony and to face the future with greater optimism. He wanted people to think well of him and to realise how valuable he was to them. On the other hand, he had a marked ability to play on the nature of individuals (such as members of the press) and was capable of advancing himself through ruthless behaviour towards them.

When he tried to come out of himself, however, he was not sure that he would be accepted by others. Fearing the loss of what he had already built, he behaved cautiously towards others. He wanted so much to measure up to other people's expectations that he tended to overestimate their material advantages as well as their human traits. Then he became intimidated because he wanted the same material things for himself. Additionally he was stimulated to match the good judgement he observed in others. He understood that everyone has weaknesses or flaws, which he could overlook when their positive traits were dominant. For example, he liked people who weren't afraid to speak their minds, provided they had something worthwhile to say. He himself could easily have been led into acts of folly by others. Perhaps as a result, he found it difficult to be free of obligations to people around him in his personal and professional affairs. Accordingly, he preferred not to be involved directly in the affairs of other people and avoided any group functions that required donations of his time and money.

TR's approach to friends was quite different from his attitude to people in general. He had a vital need for friendship and was able to influence and inspire his friends. He had a compelling need to become involved with persons who shared his strong desire for warm, sociable relationships. He was selective about making friends and was drawn to persons who were mature enough to stand on their own and who, therefore, did not need to rely on him. As a result he had an exciting array of friends ranging from the genteel to the coarse. He was perhaps intimidated by the success of his close friends, e.g. Cabot-Lodge initially and by original thinkers, but this should have aroused him to accept the challenge and try to match them. Unfortunately he experienced frequent breaks with friends due to his irritable, abrupt, self-centred and competitive traits.

Family: His early need for protection and security was supplied by his father. Unfortunately both of his parents brought him sorrow (his father died early and his mother also, at the same time as his first wife) but he believed in domestic ties and family interests. His kinder and softer side was manifested in family life. Although things were not always peaceful at home (he and his second wife did not always agree), his desire for security and the realisation of a need for caution resulted in a strong belief in guarding and cherishing those who were under his care. Thus he experienced anxiety about his inability to satisfy fully the needs of family members. Actually his children were the real catalysts in his life, stimulating him to higher levels of performance in providing for them.

Lover: TR tended to form too many intense and impressionable attachments in which he was free with his affections and unstable, possibly because of jealousy and/or a cutting harshness that led to quarrels that caused and received hurt. Harmonious conditions were possible in his sexual relationships but not easily realised. Initially, he was usually on his best behaviour, which he considered a good investment to win someone who attracted him. However, his desire for partnership was extreme, combined as it was with a restless lack of ability to be happy alone. Consequently, he had some problems in relationships and tended to attract an extravagant partner who expected too much from him. He may have had to extend himself to fulfil these expectations and thus developed an anxiety about his ability to satisfy his partner. However, once he relaxed his defence mechanisms and realised that everyone has failings, he increased his chance of forming satisfactory relationships. TR's chart clearly indicates the benefits of an early marriage (in fact, he married his first wife early following a determined pursuit) because his life could well have been influenced for good, as his powers of attachment were strong, although he himself might have been a poor marriage prospect due to his unpredictability and his attempts to break away from the conventional.

Career

Early: TR's destiny lay to some extent in his own hands in that his fortune was affected by his innate self-control, conventional notions, acquisitiveness, pride and his organising power. However, his fate depended even more on his general surroundings, circumstances, other people and, particularly, his early environment because then there was less opportunity for him to break away from early training and parental influence. His ability to succeed probably came from his parents, who taught him to assert himself within the framework of reasonable discipline and responsibility. They supported him in his struggle to make his own way. This early conditioning may also have taught him that he didn't have to get involved with others, or extend a helping hand, if he didn't want to. With this largely selfish attitude his road to success both in his career and in his relationships was likely to be paved with frustration and conflict.

It was important for him to become more self-disciplined in developing his talents to improve his competitive position. Self-development was the key and he could have become a credit to himself by building a sound mind in a sound body. It was absolutely essential that he got some formal education or his fate would have been limited indeed. He should have realised that getting an education was a good start and the first essential step towards achievement. Fortunately, learning came easily to him and he rarely forgot what he had learned. He knew he could improve his earning ability by being well-informed, so he was willing to invest in his own education. Despite the time it involved, he knew that this was the only way to exploit his creativity wisely. His desire to exploit his creativity may have been frustrated in the beginning but eventually he found the freedom to assert himself after he had learned how to be fully responsible for his actions. His success in striving for significance depended on how well he accomplished this. Deriving the most benefit from it depended on his willingness to satisfy the needs of others. Practical planning and determined self-will had united to produce brilliance in management, in science and in unusual ways. Ideals and imaginative intuitions were kept in bounds and given shape and form to make them useful practically. He found an important interest in life (politics) and developed a rather uncompromising direction to his life-effort in which he adapted his allegiances to lines along which he could make his efforts count for the most. Overall his practical nature, comprising his executive, businesslike, firm, steady and hard-working traits, would become useful to the world when he became President. When he became aware of all of this a vast world of opportunity opened up. As a result, he made a hugely valuable contribution to society, (as

President, politician, writer, scientist and explorer, etc!) and he must have accepted the responsibility for making his creativity available.

<u>Middle:</u> Because a comfortable life was important to TR, the best way to get what he wanted, and to improve the quality of life for others, was through a career that involved public service. His talent for improving existing social conditions was much needed. All he had to find was a way to make a meaningful contribution to society either through personal or group activities, and he was ready to get involved behind the scenes if necessary. Having a high regard for education he strove constantly to improve his knowledge by reading an inordinate number of learned books from around the world. Generally, he was willing to change old habits for better ones, so he was rarely locked into an attitude that might have interfered with his continuing progress. His inner and outer worlds were sufficiently well-integrated that his ambitions didn't run into any serious conflicts with his temperament. The difference between success and failure was the ability to integrate his feelings and will so that emotional distress didn't interfere with his ability to perform well in his career. His chastity (connected with his strong religious convictions) was also a key to his success because once settled and devoted he didn't have any romantic distractions. Given these factors his success was easier to achieve and he gained it fairly early in life (he became President when he was only 42).

On a cautionary note, although constructive in a narrow way, order for TR had a notable downside. His resulting mental loneliness led to fear and apprehension which, in turn, produced a lack of poise that forced brusque speech and curt writing.

Late: TR had to learn to make appropriate investments to ensure security in later life. With his abundance of ideas he could have done much to shape his future and with a little foresight his financial security and independence would have been assured, but, at times, it wasn't. Through life he had gained money, property, power and dignity, as well as gain from his partner and/or inherited money and possessions. Although he knew that his future financial security must come from using his own resources effectively, he had to discipline himself to do this. Being solvent dispelled his anxieties about the future. Potentially he did have considerable business ability with good economic management. However, he alternated between being pre-occupied with money and considering it a cross to bear. Because of that attitude he risked living on the fringes of poverty.

Health

Appearance: TR was just above average height with little that was pleasing in expression or form of body but was quick and active in all his movements. By nature he was curious, progressive, eccentric and blessed with powers of foresight. He was fond of science (biology) with some possible genius in that direction. TR enjoyed good health but in later life he became overweight.

Health: Though much may have been achieved, his tendency was to overdo everything thus impairing his vitality. He should have avoided acting hastily or on impulse, as he ran the risk of physical exhaustion. He was liable to minor accidents and possibly to moods of depression. His chart indicates the premature death of his father and an uncontroversial death for himself as a result of constitutional weakness.

Throughout his youth (and later) he suffered badly from bouts of asthma. Astrologically we can account for this by the stressful square of Mars in Scorpio to the Sun in Aquarius at Epoch. This would have been exacerbated by the effect of the afflicted Sun in Scorpio in the 6th House at birth, as well as by the effect of the minor strain aspects received by Uranus rising in Gemini, in particular from Mars, at birth. This situation of Uranus could also account for his liability to bronchitis when young. It is also significant that Taurus is rising at birth (the sign Taurus is associated with the throat) and that the Moon in Scorpio in the 5th/6th House is opposed by Uranus in Taurus at Epoch. His heart trouble, diagnosed when he was twenty, could have stemmed astrologically, once again, from the stressed situation of the Sun in Aquarius being square to Mars in Scorpio at Epoch as well as by the afflicted Sun at Birth. The effect of the opposition here of the Sun to Pluto could account for his frequent liability to diarrhoea when young.

- -

Suggestions Following from TR's Person Summary

1)   Try not to overstrain through overdoing things both physically and mentally. Physical overstrain affects vitality and mental overstrain clouds creativity and even undermines the grasp on reality.

2)   Try to guard against letting emotions, sensations and enthusiasms lead to folly through others, and to mistakes through errors of judgement. This should not be too difficult.

3)   Try to live more in the present rather than relating everything back to favourable situations in the past.

4)   Try to avoid fretful self-indulgence particularly of the 'adventures' kind. Youthful experiences enabled development of a unique identity and so became the source of mental originality. Further adventures would serve only to reinforce this.

From a present perspective and with hindsight we can suggest that as his success was due to service to the public he could have mitigated his daily schedule by delegating his responsibilities more and so could have carried on successfully, as the public fervently wished, for four more years after 1909.

References: 'The Rise of Theodore Roosevelt', 'Theodore Rex' and 'Colonel Roosevelt', E. Morris, Random House Inc., New York, USA, 1979 - 2010.

- -

CHAPTER 11

Branching Out

Throughout this book we have concentrated on Natal (equivalent to epoch plus birth) Astrology. This is basic Astrology and is the root from which Prediction, much of Electional Astrology, Synastry and Astrological Research derive. These branches all involve human life that is based on genes (DNA), with which Astrology seems so intimately connected. The temptation is to replace the word 'seems' with 'is' but perhaps we are not yet quite ready to do this.

We have concentrated on Natal Astrology because once we get this right we can then become confident that we are getting the dependent branches right also. In an attempt to keep everything as simple as possible (probably required for the evolution of life itself) we have recommended the Morinus House System as 'The House System of Choice'. We have coupled this with the 'Theory of the Pre-Natal Epoch', which fits well with our genetic understanding of our birth process. Furthermore we have recommended that we use both Epoch and Birth charts equally for interpretation purposes that then enable us to describe a person's character particularly, completely and impartially. Hence, simply by knowing the time, date and place of a person's natural birth we can describe that person's character, relationships, career and health with confidence. This seems incredible, frightening and provoking but also fascinating.

Continuing with the individual and with the Health section in particular, we have briefly examined TR's charts to see if we could identify astrological indicators for his health problems, mainly as a

140

means of supporting our choice of birth time coupled with his correct natal charts for interpretation purposes. Additionally and previously we used medical conditions (Potts' disease) to try and identify the correct Epoch chart for Alexander the Great. <u>Medical</u> Astrology should be worth much more than this (see R. C. Davison's book, p. 222). Possibly and cautiously, using the Epoch and Ideal Birth charts, we can identify and anticipate potential medical troubles from birth onwards with greater certainty. Certainly a modern replacement for H. L. Cornell's "Encyclopaedia of Medical Astrology", 1933, seems long overdue, excellent though this has been. Interested and medically qualified readers are referred to his book as an invaluable starting point.

Staying with the individual person and assuming that we really are on the right lines then we can use our accurate Epoch and Birth chart combination to describe an individual's future astrologically. This is called <u>Prediction</u>, prognostication or doing the Progressions (and Transits). Most people who ask, "Will you do my horoscope?" usually mean, "Tell me what is likely to happen to me in the future". The astrologer then assesses the future trends through which the person's life will pass. Although there have been outstanding predictions made in the past, foretelling definite events is straining deduction but certainly the person can be forewarned that certain events (both good and bad) could well be expected. Although not recommended nowadays Morin predicted the deaths of Cardinal Richelieu, Louis XIII, Wallenstein and Gustavius Adolphus within hours rather than days of their actual occurrence.

No-one has yet explained how the life of every person on Earth is connected with its two cyclic movements (its daily rotation and its yearly revolution about the Sun) but it seems to be so. The method used takes one day's movement after birth (or after epoch) as one year's development (i.e. a day for a year) of continuing life. Thus twenty five days after birth (or epoch) correspond roughly with the first twenty five years of life. The positions of the personal planets twenty five days after birth (their progressed positions) and the interpretation of the aspects that these progressed planets make with the original (and other progressed) positions make up the assessment of the trends relevant for the twenty fifth year of life. For example, long-lasting aspects made by the progressed Sun are powerful but can be "triggered" by shorter ones produced by the progressed Moon and by the progressed Morin Point. Usually the personal planets and the Morin Point change their positions significantly enough to alter their relationship with the planetary positions of the original chart over the twenty five days of the example taken. Similarly, transits (the everyday progress of the planets of the Solar System when they interact with the positions of the radical planets, i.e. day for a day progressions) can act as triggers for more long-lasting progressions and indeed can act in their own right. Once again, everything is referred back to the 'radix' (root), i.e. to the birth or epoch charts, for interpretation purposes. Importantly, we need to keep in mind that the birth and epoch charts form the underlying base from which progressions and transits are calculated and then interpreted. Readers sufficiently interested to pursue 'Prediction' are referred to M. E. Hone's book and to that of R. C. Davison entitled, "The Technique of Prediction".

Remaining with individuals, the third branch of Astrology that we can practise, although more popular in the Middle-Ages than now, is Horary Astrology. This consists of producing an astrological chart for the moment when an urgent, important question enters one's mind. Now the heavens don't arrange themselves to fit a single person's question but in moments of stress or anxiety people can feel that they become connected with something outside of themselves. Under these circumstances, "the question asks the person" rather than, "the person asks the question". The chart is cast and examined (along with the birth and epoch charts, if necessary) for the situation of the ruler of the House connected with the affairs of the question in order to provide a judgement or answer. Clearly, the question must be exact in meaning so that the right House, its mid-point and the corresponding ruler are selected for examination.   Readers sufficiently interested to follow 'Horary' further are referred to M. E. Hone's book and there to that of Raphael's 'Horary Astrology', 1931.

We can continue with individuals once more with a further branch of Astrology, namely Electional Astrology. This involves choosing a time, within a certain time-frame, for an action to be undertaken favourably.   For example, the election-date for the coronation of Queen Elizabeth I was the 15th January, 1559. Similarly, the election-date for laying the foundation stone for the Royal Observatory at Greenwich was the 10th August, 1675.

For personal matters, such as selecting the best time to retire, the person's natal charts, together with their progressions and transits, need studying in order to choose the best one of the possible times available. Sometimes the choice may require finding the lesser, or least, of two, or more, evils. In cases where an activity is planned to begin at a definite moment then the most favourable chart cast from many possible moments is based not only on favourable interplanetary positions but also when the Morin Point, relevant House and the ruler of its mid-point will be favourable. The one decided upon is called an "election map". Similarly, and with hindsight, we can see when certain "unmapped", or inceptional, beginnings were either favourable or unfortunate. Sufficiently interested readers are referred once again to M. E. Hone's book and there to that of V. Robson's, 'Electional Astrology', 1937.

Moving now from one individual to two, we compare natal charts in the activity called Synastry, meaning 'coinciding planetary influences'. Many people are anxious to confirm that they have chosen the "right" mate/partner before committing to marriage, for example, or to a business partnership. The first step is that each person studies both their own and their prospective partner's natal charts. Then the method used is to make a list of the points of likeness and difference between the charts of the one with those of the other, and vice-versa. In these lists not everything will be seen to be harmonious but if there is a real intent to make the very best of marriage or partnership then, if tactfully done, the likely causes of any disharmony can be shown, allowed for and so mitigated. Once two people realise that they do not combine well in certain ways (but well in others!), and they are prepared to admit this, they may even begin to laugh about it!

Readers interested in following Synastry further are referred to M. E. Hone's book and to that entitled 'Synastry' by R. C. Davison.

Widening our scope now to groups of people we enter the area of Astrological Research. Let us remind ourselves that we have assumed that we have the right system and that we have the accuracy of the epoch and ideal birth time chart combination to work with so that we can then apply these to studies of groups of élite professionals such as, for example (a) sports champions and (b) religious leaders. For (a) the interpretation of the personal planet Mars, involving words such as heat, energy and action, should feature strongly in the natal charts of sports champions. Although there may well be many traits that make up the character of a sports champion, those involving Mars should underlie all of them. Previously we saw that the Gauquelins rigorously and objectively detected a Mars effect in the birth charts of sports champions that Ertel confirmed. We have also reported the detection of a Mars effect by examining the Morinus birth charts of both the Gauquelins' Sports Champions Serie A and Serie D files. We have suggested that the élite professionals (i.e. sports champions in this case) not only have Mars placed favourably in their Birth charts but that this is reinforced by an additional, favourably placed Mars in their Epoch charts. Tentatively we concluded that it was this twice favourable combination that separated champions from lesser athletes and that, in general, it was this favourable combination that conferred upon new born babies the potential status of élite professional. For (b), we can imagine that the significant personal planet involved will be Venus, for its 'harmony' traits, or even the Moon for its 'response' characteristics, that will underlie any of the other characteristics that make for eminent religious leaders.

One possible advantage of Astrological Research is that we dispense with the individual Person Summaries for each of the persons in the files; we are concerned only with the overall characteristics of a particular group. On the other hand, because we are dealing with abstract characteristics, such research requires a basic knowledge of statistics to evaluate any results. The statistical distribution of planets in charts can prove difficult and finding suitable control samples can also prove unsatisfactory. In other words there are traps for the unwary in that results obtained can easily look more positive than they are in reality. For this area of study we need to be rather careful, to put it mildly.

Finally, we can widen our scope to embrace the whole 'world'. This is <u>Mundane</u> Astrology. More narrowly it means political astrology, or financial/gambling astrology or the study of the weather or of volcanic eruptions, etc. For these areas of study a much wider knowledge is required than that of Astrology alone. For Political Astrology a good knowledge of world affairs is necessary, coupled with the history of the countries involved and the Person Summaries of their leaders. A large collection of charts is required so that those applicable for any country can be accessed readily when news breaks there. Mundane astrologers need to keep up-to-date and well-informed. The maps customarily studied usually are beginnings but instead of the beginnings of lives, they are the beginnings of periods. In general we would suggest that Astrology has more relevance for life on Earth with its genes and DNA but there seems little doubt that inanimate events on Earth are also influenced by the heavenly bodies of the Solar System. Clearly Mundane Astrology is a special branch of Astrology and requires those with special aptitudes for it. Readers who find this area of Astrology particularly challenging are referred initially to M. E. Hone's book and there to that of C. E. O. Carter, 'An Introduction to Political Astrology', 1951.

<u>Eras of Time</u>.

The Great year is the name given to that period of time (about 25,800 years) that the Poles of the Earth's axis take to complete an entire circle about the Pole of the Ecliptic. This involves an oscillatory movement like that of a spinning top with a swinging motion (nutation). It is caused by the unequal gravitational pull of the Sun and the Moon upon the Earth's equatorial protuberance (the Earth is not a perfect sphere but more closely resembles an oblate spheroid). Firstly, this means that the position to which the Earth's poles point changes gradually. The nearest star to which it points is known as the Pole Star. This changes through the ages. About 4,500 years ago it pointed to Alpha Draconis, now almost to Polaris and in about 4,500 years time it will point to Alpha Cephei. Secondly, it means that the first point of Aries, as seen from the Earth each year, occurs slightly before its position in the previous one, as seen against the background of the constellations. About 2,000 years ago the first point of Aries and the start of the constellation of Aries coincided but now the first point of Aries coincides roughly with the first point of Pisces. The previous 2,000 years or so have been described as the Piscean Age so that now we are about to start the Age of Aquarius. When we speak of these Eras of Time we refer to the changing relationship between the Signs and the Constellations. However, since magnetic energy is said to enter the Earth through its Magnetic Poles the changing point of the Earth's axis may be more important and behind it we may find the cause of the differences between the twelve signs. Interested readers are referred to M. E. Hone's book, once more, and there to that of V. W. Reid, 'Towards Aquarius', 1944.

- -

ADDENDUM

Topically, if we claim to be atheists, then presumably we should be able to explain how we evolved to our present state without the need for any form of divine intervention. Previously we felt that the complexity of the carbon-based, basic life-chemical-compound, DNA, precluded the possibility that its structure could have arisen solely by chance. However, recent experiments to mimic conditions at the start of life on the Earth – Moon - Sun system about four billion years ago led to the production of RNA, a well-known precursor of DNA. This result clearly supports the atheists' cause and so enables us to proceed more confidently with our proposal that the simple Morinus system is sufficient to enable us to derive relevant Person Summaries for particular individuals by the methods we have used in this book.

If we asked atheists from when, where and how our abstract characteristics come, then possibly they would reply that they come from our genes, which, presently, is not that useful. Alternatively, we should answer that they come not only from our genes but, more usefully, also from the positions of the heavenly bodies of the Solar System and their angular interrelations with respect to the Earth, at the times of our Epoch and Birth. We may not be able to prove this to everyone's satisfaction but certainly we can have the opinion that simply and usefully, we are right. On the other hand there seems no denying that we all possess hereditary traits. Now how, when and where can these fit in . . . . . . ? (But see, for example, the last three chapters of 'Our Birth on Earth').

APPENDIX 1

Diana's Interpretations Assembled into Groups and Sections

Character

General: More objective (2c) than subjective (2b). Impulsive response to an immediate need for charity, support or help (1h). Strongly emotional and intuitive (1). Pride and self-indulgence, but great patience, perseverance and endurance (1b). Rather hard nature, great self-will, fixity of opinion and habit, somewhat combative, aggressive and alternating at times between extremes of rashness and caution, liberality and thrift (1a). Ambition and determination make high attainment possible (1e). Tendency towards headlong freedom at any price (1f). Revolutionary (1f). Individual temperament that robustly resists pigeon-holing with an individual set of purposeful emphases in her life (1g). Well-integrated personality (2). Inharmonious nature (2a). First impressions were that she was rather reserved, quiet, self-contained with some inclination for mystical or psychic pursuits (3). Inclination towards beauty and ease but too irresponsibly and carelessly (3a). A persistent, self-controlled personality capable of achieving success through hard work (1c). Practical abilities were usually combined with a shrewd mind and inner stability (1d). She was quite talented but had difficulty demonstrating it (3b). Her natural gifts could probably have been developed without external, formal training, provided she had learnt to use them efficiently (3c).

Mentality: Mentally intense, penetrative with depth of feeling and a tendency towards materialistic thought (2). There was good, commonsense mentality and nervous force (2a). Tendency towards the intangible and lack of concreteness (3a). Attracted to music, dancing, psychism, the spiritual and mystical (3b). Tendency towards all maritime matters (3c). Independence, originality and eccentricity (2e). Possibly

149

some intellectual interests with attraction for new and unusual theories (2g). Balance was shown with refined tastes and clear discrimination (2f). Led towards the occult and mystical side of life that could have awakened clairvoyant faculty (3d). Strong mental action through revolutionary thought (2e). Communicativeness could become too awkward, brusque and independent so that it lost good communication with others (2h). The addiction to the unusual and unconventional was so strong and so awkwardly expressed that she may have become eccentric, odd and tiresome (2j). Ideas were strong through heightened receptivity but likely to be carried out in a perverse, cantankerous manner with nervous strain (2i). Tendency to be self-willed, revolutionary and self-insistent (2h). Disruptive, awkward, brusque and impulsive (2h). Strong imaginative faculties (2e). Visions and ideals boundless, ethereal and inspirational but needed strength (which she had) to actualise them (3). She tended to become emotionally possessive of her thoughts that could have led her into chronic neurotic complexes that made it difficult for her to let go of the past and move clearly and freely into the future (3e). Thus she didn't understand the concept of growth fully and kept thinking herself incapable of letting go earlier phases of her life (3f). Keenly analytical approach to the organisation of her life (2d). Mind powerful, courageous, and enterprising (2b). She had a strong tendency to judge herself by her ideals while, at the same time, judged others by their actions (2c). She had a feeling of personal insecurity/inadequacy but this could have proved a spur to achievement despite obstacles (1).

Lifestyle: Conservative desire to work for the help of others, to collect and maintain family and home, coupled with difficult touchiness, quickly roused (3f). Energy spent in hard and unstinting work and expected the same from others (3c). She had no desire to preserve herself or conserve her resources (3d). She dipped deeply into life and poured forth the gathered results of her experiences with unremitting zeal (3e). She had an inclination to let matters remain as they were and to put up with them so that she became conditioned to trying circumstances but not without nervous strain (3i). Charity, help and support given

150

galvanically and unusually with personal stress (3h). Intensive personality who could not be limited to any steady point of application (2d). Her temperament was inclined to be particular yet impersonal in her interests (2c). She embarked on a practical, intense struggle for universal harmony through support, healing and charity (3a). She may have been greedy for the good things of life but this made her careless about financial resources (4). She found it difficult to hold onto her money when she was tempted to splurge on things she wanted rather than on those she really needed (4a). Probably, in this area, she needed to be more controlled (4b). She desired to become a utilitarian and to serve others (3). She kept trying to recreate her childhood so her upbringing was important to her because her childhood experiences would be carried as a residue all through her life (2a). Emotionally sensitive, she needed independence of thought and emotional security both at the same time (2b). It was likely that personal responsibilities would have been heavy with a possible inability to press forward the personal concerns in her life (3g). She tried to restore a previous image of herself (2). Accustomed to hard work she thrived on the possibility of one day looking back at jobs and projects that she had done well (3b). She tried to find an impressive and formidable identity structure that the world around her would vibrate to (1b). Something within her was lacking and she had a strong tendency to compensate (1). As a result she was learning how to stand on her own two feet and this slow process made her fearful that anybody might knock her down before she had built her own foundation (1a). Most of all she spent her life building a castle of rules that would ultimately provide the structure of the identity she wanted to achieve, which she could have succeeded in doing (1c).

Relationships

Others: She was more sociable and companionable than she appeared to be on the surface (1a). She was an inspirer but also a possible malcontent (1f). There was a love of freedom and a hatred of interference that may have extended to a headstrong disregard for the feelings of others (2). She was good in public because of her diplomatic manner (1b). She assumed that most people were freer than she was and she said so openly (2a). She had a talent for meeting people and making them feel at ease (1d). Initially she had a tendency to be careful, tactful and diplomatic (1). She was attracted to successful people, and she admired them for gaining freedom from economic worries (2b). Although she was on good social terms with everyone she met, it was her ability to understand their problems that encouraged them to request her professional skills (1e). Her way with words instantly attracted people's attention (1c). She attempted to overcome her faults through service to others, which could be declined (2f). Thus there were also frustrations in dealing with the public (2g). There were barriers between her and the people she would have liked to get close to (2d). A type of non-trusting attitude was pervasive because she had felt shut out, or closed off, from what she had tried to reach (2c). Instead of facing this she tried to be important so that others would recognise her and perhaps relate to her in a way in which she could not be hurt (2e).

Friends: She experienced frequent breaks with friends.

Family: There was the possibility of a cleavage in her life relating to parents (one of whom may have died early) and/or to early childhood as well as a spur to accomplishment (0). She easily found herself at variance with siblings, family and public, or separation from the former (2). Attractive children but could become overly possessive of loved ones (3). Possibly one of her parents died early (0a). There was an uneasy expression of affections and a lack of harmony in the home (1). If she truly cared about the people she loved, she would have tried to live up to her potential (4).

Lover: There was warmth in sexual relations (1a). Her fate was affected by marriage/love affairs, and yet she was not inclined to marriage and may well have preferred a celibate life (3). Affection was demonstrative and gay but did not want to be enchained (1). Freedom was often preferred to marriage as she tended to be too free with affections and unstable (1b). Affections and partnerships were subject to disclosures, upheavals and new starts but with trouble and unpleasantness (1c). She worried about whether she could meet the challenge of competition successfully but she found out a lot about her adversaries without their knowing it (6a). Her partner may have questioned her methods but he couldn't deny her effectiveness (6b). There were unusual conditions in marriage and partnerships (4). Changes in circumstances in both were likely to be hurtful and often unexpected (4a). Her partner's eccentricities caused exasperation (5a). She felt inhibited by a successful partner (5). The assumption of others' greater freedom was her way of defending her lack of success in competition, which really resulted from a lack of self-confidence (6). She might have married for financial gain or simply because she didn't like living alone, which were not the best reasons (3a). It would have been better to marry because she felt she had met her ideal mate (3b). Limitation of affection, or of a happy social life, had its reward in a serious, one-pointed direction (2). Love may have meant sacrifice or a life lonely except for the chosen one (2a). Partnerships will have been a serious matter but successful in a practical way (2b).

Career

<u>Early:</u> There would have been a need for an important interest in her life making for a rather uncompromising direction to her life effort (2). Her partner was probably the source of her inspiration for continually progressing to higher levels in her career (3f). Although she did need this urging she also felt that she was free to exploit her potential in her own way (3g). Gaining recognition depended entirely on her forcefulness in asserting herself despite hazards (1k). She was suitable for some official position in some public body (2k). Alternatively she would have made a good dramatic critic (4a).

Although she may have been more qualified than others she always felt that she wasn't and so not ready to take on responsibility (1c).

153

In fact she was probably over-qualified for the demands of most responsible positions (1f). She was somewhat afraid of making a fool of herself or of being caught without the necessary credentials (1d). This amounted to a powerful defence mechanism to avoid confronting a challenge (1e). If she had felt unqualified she should have got the education or training she needed (1f). She could have done much for those who lacked the resources to help themselves and so she should have chosen a career with that in mind (3). Her heart went out to those who were caught in difficult social situations and she could have accomplished much, even with modest resources, than most people would have thought possible (3b). She might have considered a career serving the public through medicine, law, psychology, vocational guidance, nutrition, self-help programs, social service, correction or institutions for the mentally or physically handicapped (2i). The important thing to remember was to find a way to implement her creative imagination and make a substantial contribution to improving society (1l). She had spent much time pondering what to do with her life and how to establish herself in a satisfying and worthwhile career (1m). She should have tried not to compare her skills with those of other people because that would have intimidated her further (1i). She mustn't have imagined that she could have achieved recognition without some sacrifices (1j). She may have had to work in obscurity at first but eventually she should have become reasonably secure (2d). Unsuccessful ambitions could have led to disappointment (1g). She needed to have been progressive in her thinking and to have tried not to belittle herself through past failures (1h). If she had looked ahead she would have realised that with a little planning she could have established and achieved her goals but her dream needed to have been a vivid one (1n). Working with the public could have been the key to her success and fulfilment but it would have involved many responsibilities (2g). The demands of her career may have limited her freedom but through her accomplishments she would have eventually gained the public's respect and her own greater freedom (2h). Her destiny would have been served by helping to fulfil the needs of the public (2b). Public relations might have been a comfortable field for her relatively benign nature (2c). She was more suitable for external activities rather than for an indoor occupation (2f). She had ability for painting and general artistic faculties (4). With the right training she might have found that serving people had its own rewards, especially if she had offered professional services (2a).

Investment counselling, insurance, retirement counselling, or family counselling were some areas in which she could have found ample opportunities to succeed and have the chance to express her creative talent fully (2j). Her partner should have been willing to share the lean years with her until she had become established and reached the goals she had defined earlier (3h). Importantly she had had to define them so that she would have been properly motivated for that objective (3i). She underestimated her abilities and thus failed to capitalise on them (1b). Her fear of risks made it difficult for her to exploit her creative potential fully (1a). She underestimated her ability to make an important contribution to society (1b). She was extremely sensitive to human frailty and knew how to solve the problems it caused (3a). Circumstances would affect her much more than her ability to make her own destiny (1). She was better organising things than people (2f). She was a good worker at following past, established procedures (2e).

<u>Middle:</u> She could patiently reach a conclusion but not with ease (1g). Results had to be battled for (1h). The narrowness engendered produced selfishness and egocentricity (1i). Hardness was endured and sternness given (1j). She adapted her allegiances to lines along which she could make her efforts count for the most (1m). The tendency was that her magnetic determination conduced to results through strength of personality and self-belief (1n). Support, help and useful work was given humanely and unusually to some of the most unfortunate members of society (2a). Tendency that she had to meet people on mutually agreeable terms and that she took advantage of every opportunity to earn a reasonable income (1l). Probably she would have earned her living by working with the public (1). Her talent allowed her to serve

people's needs (1b). Achieving significance in her life efforts required focussing on the affairs of others, either personally or professionally (1a). It was necessary for her to concern herself with the public's requirements (1c). Fortunately she must have had every resource she needed to satisfy this kind of responsibility, but she may have been apprehensive about the value of applying her talents in this way (1d). Her feelings of insecurity may have forced her to avoid making a commitment because she didn't want to risk losing what she had already gained (1e). She felt that others could help themselves as she had and she resented it when others wanted her always to be available to them (1k). Commendably her efforts made their future security possible (2b). She knew that they would happily do favours for her in return, if necessary (2c). The expression of herself in carefulness, practical ability, patience and success by long and ambitious planning was likely to come to its fruition (1f). She was capable of locking out interference and of directing her life towards a useful purpose enabling her to achieve so much (1o). She worked backwards, i.e. not starting anything until she could visualise the finished product (1p). Her practical approach to life increased (1q). She was especially good at picking up pieces from the past that society had overlooked and making a great life's work out of such seemingly useless fragments, probably because she could not tolerate waste (2). The amount of inner meaning these achievements brought to her was the most important thing to her (2d). She would have become ready to bring to fruition much labour along a given path (1r).

Health

She had robust health (1) but liable to feverish complaints (1g). Danger of accidents by burns, scalds and falls (1h). Physical overstrain was risked (1e). Eyesight may have needed protection (1b). She was a good sleeper (1d). She was subject to moods of depression (1f). Nervous system strengthened, hence good eyesight (1a), hearing and touch (1c). There was the possibility of a sudden, quick and painful death in a public place (2).

- -

APPENDIX 2

Diana's Synthesised and Blended Interpretations in Order

Character

General: Strongly emotional and intuitive, she had a rather hard nature, great self-will, fixity of habit and opinion together with a somewhat combative disposition that alternated between extremes of rashness and caution. She had pride and self-indulgence but also much patience, perseverance, persistence, self-control and endurance that was capable of achieving success through hard work. Practical abilities were combined with a shrewd mind and inner stability. Ambition and determination made high attainment possible. However, she also had a revolutionary tendency to pursue headlong freedom at any price.

She had an individual temperament that robustly resisted pigeon-holing, with a set of purposeful emphases in her life. Although she was a well-integrated personality she had a somewhat inharmonious nature that may have experienced difficulty making decisions. On first meeting she appeared to be rather reserved, quiet and self-controlled but, despite appearances, she was highly sensitive inside. There were also inclinations towards 1) beauty, art, dancing, music and taking life easily but too irresponsibly and carelessly and 2) maritime, mystical and psychic pursuits. Overall she was quite talented but had difficulty showing it. Probably her natural gifts could have been developed without external, formal training, provided she had learnt to use them efficiently.

Mentality: Diana had a feeling of personal insecurity/inadequacy but this could have proved a spur to achievement despite obstacles. She was mentally intense, penetrative with depth of feeling and a tendency towards materialistic thought. Possibly this strong mental action included some intellectual interests with an attraction towards new and unusual ideas. She had a good commonsense mentality and nervous force. Her

158

forceful, courageous and enterprising mind made her judge herself by her ideals, while, at the same time, judging others by their actions. She had a keenly analytical approach to the organisation of her life. Balance was evident with refined tastes and clear discrimination. However, communication of revolutionary thought and strong intuitions could have become too awkward, brusque and independent so that it lost good contact with others and became tiresome. Additionally she had a tendency to the intangible, which evoked in her boundless and inspirational ideals and visions that needed her mental strength to actualise them. On balance, she tended to become emotionally possessive of her thoughts that could have led her into chronic, neurotic complexes that made it difficult for her to let go of the past and move clearly and freely into the future. As a result she didn't fully appreciate the idea of growth and kept thinking herself incapable of letting go of earlier phases of her life.

Lifestyle: Something within her was lacking and she had a strong tendency to compensate. She was learning how to stand on her own two feet but this slow process made her fearful that anybody may knock her down before she had built up her own foundation. She tried to find an impressive and formidable identity structure that the world around her could vibrate to. Most of all she spent her life building a castle of rules that ultimately would provide the structure for this identity that she wanted to achieve, which she could well have succeeded in doing.

She kept trying to restore a previous, childhood image of herself. This meant that her upbringing was important to her because her childhood experiences would be carried as a residue all through her life. Emotionally sensitive, she had needed independence of thought as well as emotional security, simultaneously, while she was growing up.

Her temperament was inclined to be particular in her interests yet also impersonal. As an intense personality, who could not be limited to any steady point of application, she desired to become utilitarian and to serve others. She embarked on a practical, intense struggle for widespread harmony through support, healing and charity. Accustomed to hard work she thrived on the possibility of one day looking back at jobs and projects that she had done well. Energy was spent in hard and unstinting work and she expected the same from others. She had little desire to preserve herself or to conserve her resources. She dipped deeply into life and poured forth the gathered results of her experiences with unremitting zeal. Her conservative desire to work for the help of others, as well as to collect and maintain family and home resulted in difficult touchiness, quickly roused. Accordingly, personal responsibilities would have been heavy with a possible inability to press forward the personal concerns of her life. This may well have led to an inclination to let difficulties remain as they were and put up with them so that she became conditioned to trying circumstances but not without nervous stress. Thus charity, support and help tended to be provided impulsively, magnetically and unusually yet involving personal strain.

In addition she may have been greedy for the good things of life but this made her careless with her financial resources. She then found it difficult to hold onto her money when she was tempted to splurge on things she wanted rather than on those she really needed. Probably, in this area, she needed to be more controlled.

Relationships

Others: Her initial approach to meeting people was careful, tactful and diplomatic but she was more sociable and companionable within than she appeared on the surface. She was good in public because of her diplomatic manner and her way with words instantly attracted people's attention Thus she had a talent for meeting people and making them feel at ease. But although she was on good social terms with everyone she met it was her ability to understand their problems that encouraged them to request her professional skills. She was an inspirer of others but also a possible malcontent. There was a love of freedom and a hatred of interference that may have extended to a headstrong disregard for the feelings of others. She assumed that most people were

160

freer than she was and she said so openly. Although she was attracted to successful people, whom she admired for gaining freedom from economic worries, a type of non-trusting attitude was pervasive because she had felt shut out, or closed off from, what she had tried to reach. Hence there were barriers between her and the people she would like to get close to. Instead of facing this she tried to be important so that others would recognise her and perhaps relate to her in a way in which she could not be hurt. She tried to overcome her difficulties through service to others, which could have been declined. Consequently there were frustrations as well as successes when dealing with people.

Friends: Diana experienced frequent breaks with friends.

Family: There was the possibility of a cleavage in Diana's life relating to parents (one of whom may have died early) and/or to early childhood. She had an uneasy expression of affection and there was a lack of harmony at home. She easily found herself at odds with siblings, family and public, or separation from the former. She had attractive children and could have become overly possessive of loved ones. If she had truly cared for the people she loved she would have tried to live up to her potential.

Lover: Diana's affections were demonstrative, lively and there was warmth in sexual relations but she didn't want to be enchained. She may have preferred freedom to marriage tending to be too free with her affections and unstable. Her partnerships and affections were subject to disclosures, upheavals and new starts but with trouble and unpleasantness. However, limitation of affection, or of a happy social life, had its reward in a serious, single-minded direction. Love may have meant sacrifice, or a life lonely except for the chosen one. Such partnerships would have been a serious matter but successful in a practical way. Her fate was affected by marriage or love affairs, and yet she was not that inclined to marriage and may well have preferred a celibate life. She might have married for financial gain, or simply because she didn't like living alone, which were not the best reasons. She would have done better to marry because she had met her ideal mate.

Unusual conditions existed in her marriage and partnerships. Changes in circumstances in both were likely to be hurtful and unexpected. She felt intimidated by a successful partner and his eccentricities caused exasperation. Her assumption of others' greater freedom was her way of defending her lack of success in competition, which really resulted from a lack of self-confidence. She worried about whether she could successfully meet the challenges of competition and she found out a lot about her adversaries without them knowing it. Her partner may have questioned her methods but he couldn't deny her effectiveness.

Career

Early: Circumstances would rule Diana much more than her ability to make her own destiny. Her fear of risks made it difficult for her to exploit her creative potential. She underestimated her ability to make an important contribution to society and so failed to capitalise on it. Although she may have been more talented than others she always felt that she wasn't and so not ready to take on responsibility. She was somewhat afraid of making a fool of herself or of being caught without the necessary credentials. This amounted to a powerful defence mechanism to avoid confronting a challenge. In fact she was probably sufficiently talented for the demands of most responsible positions but if she had felt unqualified then she should have got the education or training she needed. Unsuccessful early ambitions could have led to disappointment. She needed to be progressive in her thinking and have tried not to belittle herself because of past failures. She should have tried not to compare her skills with those of other people because that would have intimidated her further. She mustn't have imagined that she could have achieved recognition without some sacrifices. Gaining recognition depended entirely on her own forcefulness in asserting herself despite hazards. The important thing to remember was to find a way to implement her creative imagination and make a substantial contribution.

She had spent much time pondering what to do with her life and how to establish herself in a satisfying and worthwhile career. If she had looked ahead she would have realised that with a little planning she could have defined and achieved her goals so that she would have been properly motivated but her dream needed to have been a vivid one.

There would have been a need for an important interest in her life making for a rather uncompromising direction to her life-effort. With the right training she might have found that serving people had its own rewards especially if she had offered professional services. Her destiny would have been served by helping to fulfil the needs of the public. Indeed public relations might have been a comfortable field for her relatively benign nature. She may have had to work in obscurity at first but eventually she would have become reasonably secure. She was a good worker at following past, established procedures and better at organising things than people. She was more suitable for external activities than for a life indoors. Working with the public would have been the key to her success and fulfilment but it would have involved many responsibilities. Had she shown sufficient intellectual ability she might have considered a career serving the public through medicine, law, psychology, vocational guidance, nutrition, self-help programs, social service, correction or institutions for the mentally or physically handicapped. Investment counselling, insurance, retirement or family counselling comprised some extra areas in which she could have found ample opportunities to succeed and have the chance to express her talent fully.

She could have done much for those who lacked the resources to help themselves and so she could have chosen a career with that in mind. She was extremely sensitive to human frailty and knew how to solve the problems it caused. Her heart went out to those who were caught in difficult social situations and she could have accomplished much, even with modest resources, than most people would have thought possible.

She had ability for painting, music and dancing with a general artistic aptitude. She could have made a good drama critic.

Middle: Probably Diana would have earned her living by working with people. She would have achieved significance in her life-efforts by focussing on the affairs of others either personally or professionally. Hence it was necessary for her to allow her talents to serve the public's concerns. Fortunately she had every resource she needed to satisfy this kind of responsibility but she may have been apprehensive about the value of applying her efforts in this way. Her feelings of insecurity may have caused her to avoid making a commitment because she didn't want to risk losing what she had already gained. The expression of herself in carefulness, practical ability and patience coupled with long and ambitious planning had brought success but not with ease. Results had had to be battled for through care and patience. The nervousness engendered had produced selfishness and egocentricity. Hardness had been endured and sternness had resulted. She felt that others could help themselves as she had and she resented it when others wanted her always to be available to them. The tendency was that she had to meet people on mutually agreeable terms and that she took advantage of every opportunity to earn a reasonable income. Thus she adapted her allegiances to lines along which she could make her efforts count for the most. The tendency was also that her magnetic determination conduced to results through strength of personality and belief in herself. She was capable of locking out interference and of directing her life towards a useful purpose enabling her to achieve so much. She worked backwards, i.e. she never started anything until she could visualise the finished product. Her practical approach to life increased and she would have become ready to bring to fruition much labour along a given path.

Diana was especially good at picking up pieces from the past that society had overlooked and making a great life's work out of such seemingly useless fragments, probably because she could not tolerate waste. Support, help and useful work was given humanely, unusually and impulsively to some of the most unfortunate members of society.

Commendably her efforts made their future security possible. She knew that they would happily do favours for her, on return, if necessary. The amount of inner meaning these achievements brought to her was the most important thing to her.

Health

Diana had good health and a strong nervous system; and good eyesight (despite a possible need for protection), hearing and sense of touch. She was a good sleeper but she risked physical overstrain and was subject to moods of depression. She was liable to feverish complaints, to accidents by burns and scalds and to falls. Unfortunately there was an indication of a sudden, quick and painful death in a public place.

- -

APPENDIX 3

TR's Interpretations Assembled into Groups and Sections

Character

General: Objective (1), Inclined to peevish and fretful self-indulgence (3), Remorseful (3a), humble, patient (2a), Discontented, unhappy (2b). Industry, thrift, perseverance, economy (2d). Feeling of personal insecurity/ inadequacy (2). Somewhat worldly and selfish nature, self-assertive, proud (1c). Very strong willed, and not easily influenced or turned aside (1d). Irritability, abruptness or aggressiveness possible (1f). Pugnacious and bad-tempered (1e). Endurance stimulated (1d). Love of travel and good food (3a). Drive and careful consideration (2c). His otherwise harmonious personality was drawn to mistakes through his feelings and sensations (1h). He had a hard and practical nature that necessitated his involvement with the world and mixing with men (1). Moody or quarrelsome nature (1g). Some ambition with an inclination to run in a groove (1a), or become too conventional and tending to an over-cautious approach (2e). Love of the easy, the beautiful and the pleasant at any price, but a tougher note was provided by the other parts of his nature (3a). Well-integrated personality (1b).

Mentality: Intelligent (1a). Was able to get to the bottom of problems (3a). Limitations through maze-like worries but these cleared up in the long run through patient endurance and quiet keeping out of the limelight (3c). Ideas and intuitions strong through heightened receptivity but might have been carried out in a perverse of cantankerous manner with nervous tension (1b). Psychic and mystical tendencies awakened but also control of his sensations (4b). Utilitarian outlook stimulated as well as pensiveness and the ability to 'merge' ideas (3). More determination, love of power and ambition but also less internal receptivity (1). Contemplative thought and deeply religious (4b). Possible psychic and

166

occult tendencies (4b). Secretive, penetrative and passionate traits emphasised (4a). Spiritual pleasures were a joy and happiness but not always satisfied harmoniously (4). Wise control, caution and commonsense in all correspondence, communication, education or literary work (3b). Formal education scanty (1a). He tried to express himself as quickly and as spontaneously as he could all the time (2a). Highly active mental life (2). He tried to find the identity that made him the most comfortable (2f). He strove to establish his own uniqueness so that he could distinguish his own identity from the myriad of identities he saw around him (2g). He had little interest in the rules and traditions of the society he lived in and identified with that which was new and unique rebelling against being caged or pigeon-holed (2h). As he was nervous and erratic he was highly influenced by all the available external thought in the world (2i). This made it difficult for him to stick to any one topic, or project, for any length of time (2k). His interest in exploring all mental possibilities made life a mishmash of scattered ideas and attitudes (2j). Without enough confidence in his own uniqueness of thought he tended to identify with the originality of others. (2l). There was a distinct danger that he could actually lose his reality perspective but he did have control and idealism here to keep his feet on the ground (2m). Otherwise he could easily have been thrown away from any realistic goal-oriented approach to life (2n). Unconsciously he was highly gullible and so needed to avoid hypnosis or other deep-mind techniques which would have tended to take him too quickly into levels of his being that he would not have been ready to handle (2o). In fact he was so mentally activated that even his strong interest in sexuality took on more of mind exploration than it did any physical or emotional fulfilment (2b). As one of the most curious of people he was the investigator who could not decide on any given chosen path as being the right one for him (2c). He tried very many different things but never really settled on any one of them (2d). Consequently he knew people from many different walks of life, each one coming from something that he himself would have liked to try (2e). One day he may have come to realise that the mental gymnastics he had been using for decades had basically been keeping him from experiencing himself (2s). Consequently he continued to explore worlds that were wider and with more possibilities than anything he had experienced before (2r). As a first-class seeker he sacrificed much of the comforts of traditional society so that he could be free to discover that which existed just beyond the limits of his contemporaries (2q). Change was continuous until he understood that his true purpose was not to dedicate his life to any principle or course of action because that would have smothered his spirit of adventure (2p).

Lifestyle: He had no desire to preserve himself or to conserve his resources (3). He dipped deeply into life and poured forth the result of his gathered experiences with unremitting zeal (2). He put up with difficulties, thereby becoming conditioned to trying circumstances but not without nervous strain (6a). Personal responsibilities were heavy (6). He had a lack of power to express himself in creative, happy ways (5b). Enjoyment of life did not come easily (5c). He dwelt on emotions which had burdened him in his early years during which he had a high need for security (8). He tended to stifle his emotions in as if to save them for the one individual he may have met in the future who would have been symbolic of the past security he had lost (8a). When travelling he would keep identifying each new place with a past he was already comfortable in (8b). In this way he could move through life with a feeling that he was securely rooted, no matter where, or with whom, he was (8c). Because he experienced living in a changing world it would have been better, if instead of trying to make his present life fit into his past, he realised and accepted it within the past security he had known so that he no longer had to seek it continually in the outer world (8d). He tried to find an impressive and formidable identity structure that the world around him could vibrate to (8h). Something within him was lacking and he had a strong tendency to compensate (8e). There were barriers between him and the people he would have liked to get close to (8f). A type of non-trusting attitude was pervasive because he had felt shut out, or closed off, from what he had tried to reach (8g). Instead of facing this problem he

168

tried to be important so that others would recognise him, and perhaps relate to him in a way in which he could not be hurt (8h). Highly sensitive inside, despite external appearances, he was learning how to stand on his own two feet and this slow process made him fearful that anybody may knock him down before he had built his own foundations (8i). Love of ease and inactivity but need to be careful that business interests were not sacrificed to home cares and that public interests were not sacrificed for personal gain (8k). He attempted to adjust to difficulties and to by-pass them but rarely without nervous tension (6a). He had to reserve enough time for himself so that he could unwind and enjoy some of the benefits that he had deserved (8j). He had a unique ability to remain relatively unaffected by the lifestyle of those around him (5). His cool detachment may have caused him some anxiety later on because he didn't plan ahead, assuming that everything would turn out well (5a). He tended to function largely on nervous energy and he wanted to do everything right away, because he never knew what would happen tomorrow (1). His keen perception told him what was right or wrong with the politics of his time, so he could well have become involved in this area (4).

Relationships

Others: He was able to deal with people (1). He had a talent for helping people achieve greater harmony and face the future with greater optimism (1d). When he tried to come out of himself he was not sure that that he would have been fully accepted by others (2). He was stimulated to match the good judgement he observed in others (2d). He had great ability for playing on the nature of others (3c). He found it difficult to be free of obligations to people around him in his personal and professional affairs (3a). He could have been led easily into acts of folly by others (3). He had a tendency to advance himself through ruthless behaviour towards others (3d). Fearing the loss of his resources he asserted himself cautiously towards others (2a). He preferred not to be

169

involved in the affairs of other people so he avoided any group functions that required donations of his time and money (3b). He wanted so much to measure up to other people's expectations that he tended to overestimate their material advantages as well as their human traits (2b). Then he became intimidated because he wanted the same things for himself (2c). He understood that everyone has weaknesses or flaws, which he could overlook when their positive traits were outstanding (2e). Generally he was willing to help others with their problems (1a). He may have been motivated by a strong spiritual commitment to serve others, in which case his results were much greater than the sacrifices he had made for them (1c). He enjoyed people who weren't afraid to speak their minds, provided they had something worthwhile to say (2f). There was a love of support, help and charity given humanely to the contemporary lowest priorities of society (1b).

Friends: He was selective about making friends (2). He was drawn to persons who were mature enough to stand on their own (3). There were frequent breaks with friends (6). He might have been intimidated by the success of his close friends but this should have aroused him to accept the challenge and try to match them (5). He had a vital need for friendship and was able to influence friends (1). He had an exciting array of friends, ranging from the genteel to the coarse (4). He had a compelling need to become to become involved with persons who shared his strong desire for warm, sociable relationships (1a).

Family: There was anxiety about his ability to indulge family members satisfactorily (3a). His desire for security and the realisation of a need for caution resulted in a strong feeling for guarding and cherishing those who were under his care (3b). There may have been sorrow through either of his parents (1). TR believed in domestic ties, and family interests (2). He had a kinder and softer side in social matters (2b) and in family life (2a). His children were the real catalysts in his life stimulating him to higher levels of performance in providing for them (3c). There was a lack of peace at home (3).

<u>Lover/Partner:</u>   There was anxiety about his ability to indulge his partner (1j). Once he had relaxed his defence mechanisms and realised that everyone had failings, he increased the chance of having satisfactory relationships (1k).   Jealousy (1d).   Usually a permanent relationship was the best way for two people in love to fulfil their needs for each other, and that didn't mean that one was using the other, except in mutual interest (2).   He formed impressionable attachments (1b).   Quiet devotion that was unassuming and considerate. An early marriage was recommended because his life might have been influenced for good as his powers of attachment were very strong (2a). He may have had some problems in relationships; he may have attracted a partner who expected a lot from him so that he really had to extend himself to satisfy her expectations (1i). He was too free with affection and unstable (1c). Harmonious conditions in sexual relationships but not easily realised (1f). He was usually on his best behaviour, which he considered a good investment to win someone who attracted him (1g). He had too many love affairs (1). His desire for partnership was overdone with a restless lack of ability to be happy alone (1h). There was a tendency that a cutting harshness entered affections (1). He experienced intense sexual relations but with quarrels (1a). His feelings were strong but caused and received hurt (1e).   He presented a poor situation for marriage due to his unpredictability and to his attempts to break away from the conventional (2b).

Career

<u>Early:</u> His destiny was supplied by fate, circumstances and others (1a). He had an important interest in life and a rather uncompromising direction to his life-effort (2q). He adapted his allegiances to lines along which he could make his effort count for the most (2r). It was important for him to become more self-disciplined in developing his talents to improve his competitive position (2). Learning came easily to him and he rarely forgot what he had learned (2g). He valued education as the first

essential step towards achievement (2e). He knew that this was the only way to exploit his creativity wisely (2h). Practical planning and determined self-will united to produce brilliance in management, in science and in unusual ways (2n). Ideals and imaginative intuitions were kept in bounds and given shape and focus to make them useful practically (2o). His practical nature could be useful in the world for executive, business-like, firm, steady and hard-working purposes for prominence and responsibility (2p). Deriving the most benefit from his fine creativity depended on his willingness to satisfy the needs of others (2m). His early conditioning may have taught him that he didn't have to get involved with others, or extend a helping hand, if he didn't want to (1f). With this attitude his road to success would have been paved with frustration and conflict (1g). His fate depended on environmental and general surroundings and was influenced by conventional notions, acquisitiveness and pride (1b). His destiny was somewhat in his own hands (1). His ability to succeed probably came from his parents, who taught him how to assert himself within the framework of reasonable discipline and responsibility (1d). They supported him in his struggle to make his own way (1e). His success in striving for significance depended on how well he accomplished this (2l). He could have made a valuable contribution to society, and he must have had to accept the responsibility for making his creativity available (2i). A vast world of opportunity opened up when he became aware of this (2j). His desire to exploit his creativity may have been frustrated in the beginning but eventually he would have found the freedom to assert himself, when he had learned how to be fully responsible for his actions (2k). Self-development was the key (2a). He could have become a credit to himself by building a sound mind in a sound body (2b). He knew he could improve his earning ability by being well-informed, so he was willing to invest in getting an education (2f). His fate depended on his early environment because there was less power for him to break away from early training and parental influence (1c). His fortune was affected by his innate self-control and his organising power (1). As painful as it seems he really should have got some formal education or his future would have seemed limited indeed (2c). He should have realised that getting an education was a good start (2d).

<u>Middle:</u>   Although constructive in a narrow, one-track way, order could become dreary planning (2). Mental loneliness resulted because of fear and apprehension producing a lack of poise and so forced brusque speech and writing (2a). He knew that his future financial security must come from using his own resources effectively (3e). He was likely to gain money, property, power or dignity (3g). Because a comfortable lifestyle was important to him, the best way to get what he wanted and to improve the quality of life for others was through a career that involved public service (1).   He had to learn to make appropriate investments to ensure security later in life (3). He had to discipline himself to make the most of his basic resources (3d). Being solvent dispelled his anxieties about the future (3c). He had considerable business ability that earned or inherited money or property, with good economic management (3h). Generally he was willing to change old habits for better ones, so he was rarely locked into an attitude that might have interfered with his continuing progress (1e). His inner and outer worlds were sufficiently well-integrated so that his ambition didn't run into any serious conflicts with his temperament (1f). Because of these considerations success would have been easier to achieve, and he should have gained it fairly early in life (1i). He had to find a way to make a meaningful contribution to society either through personal, or group, activities (1b). His talent for improving existing social conditions was much needed (1a). He was ready to work behind the scenes if necessary (1c). Having a high regard for education he strove constantly to increase his knowledge (1d). There was gain through his partner's money, or inherited money or possessions but not satisfied harmoniously (3f). He alternated between being preoccupied with money and considering it a cross to bear (3i). Because of that attitude he may have been on the fringe of poverty (3j). His chastity was also a key to his success (1h). The difference between success and failure was the ability to integrate his feelings and will so that emotional distress didn't interfere with his ability to perform well in his own career (1g). With

his abundance of ideas he could have done much to shape his future (3a). With a little foresight his financial security and independence would have been assured (3b).

Health

Possible moods of depression (2c). Premature death of father (2d). Though much may have been achieved his tendency was to overstrain through overdoing thereby impairing his vitality (2). Liable to minor accidents (2b). An easy, honourable death through constitutional weakness (2e). Rather short stature (1). Nothing pleasing in expression or form of body (1c). Good health both from nutrition and digestion (1g). The size of his body was increased resulting in stoutness (1h). He should have avoided acting hastily or on impulse, otherwise he ran the risk of physical exhaustion (2a). Tall stature (1a). Extravagant partner. Fond of science (1f). Curious, reforming, progressive, foreseeing and eccentric (1e). Quick and active in all his movements (1d). Possibly extravagant partner (1i).

APPENDIX 4

TR's Synthesised and Blended Interpretations in Order

Character

General: There appear to be two sides to TR's character. Firstly, he had a hard, practical and objective nature that necessitated his involvement with the world and mixing with men but he had an inclination to live in a groove. His well-integrated but somewhat worldly, ambitious and selfish nature was too positive, self-reliant, self-assertive and proud. His very strong, enduring will was not easily influenced or turned aside but when thwarted he could become irritated, abrupt, moody, quarrelsome, bad-tempered and pugnacious. As a result his otherwise stable personality was drawn to mistakes through his feelings and sensations.

On the other hand, and at the same time, he had a feeling of personal insecurity/inadequacy that produced discontent, unhappiness, thrift, economy, conventionality, humility and careful consideration. In between these two sides, or perhaps because of them, he was inclined to fretful, peevish self-indulgence possibly followed by remorse. There was a love of the easy, good food, travel, the beautiful and the pleasant almost at any price but, as we have seen, a tougher note was provided by other parts of his nature.

Mentality: TR had determination, love of power and ambition but at the expense of interpersonal sensitivity. Despite his scanty formal education there is no doubt that TR was intelligent. His ideas and intuitions were strong through heightened receptivity but could have been carried out in a perverse or cantankerous manner with nervous tension. He was so highly active mentally that he tried to express himself as quickly and as spontaneously as possible all the time. Even his strong

175

sexuality took on more of a mind exploration than it did any physical or emotional fulfilment. As one of the most curious people he was the investigator who could not decide upon any chosen path as being the right one for himself. He tried very many different careers but never really settled on any one of them. Consequently he knew many different people from many walks of life, each one coming from an area that he himself would have liked to try. He tried to find the identity that made him the most comfortable. He strove to establish his own uniqueness so that he could distinguish his own identity from the myriad of identities he met around him. He had little interest in the rules and traditions of the society he lived in and identified with all that was new and unique, rebelling against being caged or pigeon-holed. As he was nervous and erratic he was highly influenced by all the available external thought in the world. His interest in exploring all mental possibilities tended to make his mind a mishmash of scattered ideas and attitudes. This made it difficult for him to stick to any one topic, or project, for any length of time. As a result he lacked confidence with the uniqueness of his own thoughts and tended to identify with the originality of others. There was a distinct danger that he could actually lose his reality perspective but here he did have control and idealism to keep his feet on the ground. Otherwise he could easily have become diverted from any goal-minded approach to life. Unconsciously he was highly gullible and so needed to avoid hypnosis or other deep-mind techniques which would have tended to take him too quickly into levels of his being that he would not have been ready to handle.

Change was continuous for him until he understood that his true purpose was not to dedicate his life to any principle or course of action because that would have smothered his spirit of adventure. As a determined, even selfish explorer of the meaning of his own personal existence, he sacrificed much of the comforts of traditional society so that he could be free to discover that which existed just beyond the limits of his contemporaries. Thus he continued to explore worlds that were wider and contained more possibilities than anything he had explored before.

One day he may have come to realise that all his mental gymnastics, that he had been using for decades, had been keeping him from experiencing himself.

Additionally his utilitarian outlook, pensiveness and his ability to merge ideas were stimulated. He became able to see to the bottom of problems. He exercised wise control, caution and commonsense in all correspondence, communication, education or literary work. Distraction did occur through maze-like worries but these cleared up in the long run through patient endurance and quiet keeping out of the limelight.

Spiritual and religious pleasures were a joy and happiness but not always satisfied harmoniously. His secretive, passionate and penetrative traits were emphasised. Possibly his psychic, occult and mystical tendencies were awakened but also his control of them.

Lifestyle: TR tended to function largely on nervous energy and he wanted to do everything right away because he never knew what would happen tomorrow. He dipped deeply into life and poured forth the result of his gathered experiences with unremitting zeal. He had no desire to preserve himself or to conserve his resources. His keen perception told him what was right or wrong with contemporary politics, so he could well have become involved in this area. He had a unique ability to remain relatively unaffected by the lifestyles of those around him. His cool detachment may have caused him some anxiety later on because he didn't plan ahead, assuming that everything would turn out well. There may have been a lack of power to express himself in creative, happy ways, so that despite himself, his enjoyment of life did not come easily. Personal responsibilities were heavy. As a result he attempted to put up with, to adjust to, or to by-pass difficulties, thereby becoming conditioned to trying circumstances but rarely without nervous strain. He dwelt on emotions which had burdened him in his early years during which he had had a high need for security. He tended to stifle his emotions in as if to save them for the one individual he may meet in the future who would be symbolic of the past security now lost to him. When travelling he would

177

keep identifying each new place with a past that he was already comfortable in. In this way he could move through life with the feeling that he was securely rooted, no matter where he was, or whom he was with. Because he experienced living in a changing world it would have been better if instead of trying to make his present life fit into his past, he realised and accepted it within the past security he had known, so that he no longer had to seek them continually in the outer world.

Something within him was lacking and he tried hard to compensate. There were barriers between him and the people he would have liked to get close to. A type of non-trusting attitude was pervasive because he had felt shut out, or closed off from, what he had tried to reach. Instead of facing this problem he tried to be important by finding an impressive and formidable identity structure that the world around him could vibrate to, so that others would recognise him, and perhaps relate to him in a way that he could not be hurt. Despite external appearances he was highly sensitive inside. He was learning how to stand on his own two feet and this slow process made him fearful that anybody might knock him down before he had built his own foundation. Somehow he had to reserve enough time for himself so that he could unwind and enjoy some of the benefits that he had deserved. In fact a part of him had a love of ease and inactivity but he needed to be careful that business or public interests weren't sacrificed either to home cares or to personal gain.

Relationships

Others: TR was able to deal with people and generally he was willing to help others with their problems. There was a love of support, help and charity given humanely to the contemporary lowest priorities of society. He may have been motivated by a strong spiritual commitment to serve others, in which case his results were much greater than the sacrifices he had made for them. In fact he had a talent for helping people achieve greater harmony and face the future with greater optimism.

When he tried to come out of himself he was not sure that he would have been accepted by others. Fearing the loss of his resources he asserted himself cautiously towards others. He wanted so much to measure up to other peoples' expectations that he tended to overestimate their material advantages as well as their human traits. Then he became intimidated because he wanted the same things for himself. Additionally he was stimulated to match the good judgement he observed in others. He understood that everyone has weaknesses or flaws, which he could overlook when their positive traits were outstanding. For example, he enjoyed people who weren't afraid to speak their minds, provided they had something worthwhile to say. He himself could easily have been led into acts of folly by others. Perhaps as a result, he found it difficult to be free of obligations to people around him in his personal and professional affairs. Accordingly, he preferred not to be involved in the affairs of other people and avoided any group functions that required donations of his time and money. On the other hand, he had a great ability in playing on the nature of others with a tendency to advance himself through ruthless behaviour towards them.

Friends: TR had a vital need for friendship and was able to influence his friends. He had a compelling need to become involved with persons who shared his strong desire for warm, sociable relationships. He was selective about making friends and was drawn to persons who were mature enough to stand on their own. As a result he had an exciting array of friends ranging from the genteel to the coarse. He might have been intimidated by the success of his close friends but this should have aroused him to accept the challenge and try to match them. Unfortunately he experienced frequent breaks with friends.

Family: His early need for protection and security was supplied by his father. Unfortunately there was sorrow through both of his parents but

179

he believed in domestic ties and family interests. He had a kinder and softer side in family life and in social matters. Although things were not always peaceful at home his desire for security and the realisation of a need for caution resulted in a strong feeling for guarding and cherishing those who were under his care. Thus he experienced anxiety about his ability to indulge family members satisfactorily. Actually his children were the real catalysts in his life stimulating him to higher levels of performance in providing for them.

Lover: TR tended to form too many, intense, and impressionable attachments in which he was free with his affections and unstable, possibly because of jealousy and/or a cutting harshness led to quarrels that caused and received hurt. Harmonious conditions were possible in sexual relationships but not easily realised. He was usually on his best behaviour, which he considered a good investment to win someone who attracted him. His desire for partnership was overdone with a restless lack of ability to be happy alone. Consequently, he had some problems in relationships and he may have attracted a partner who expected a lot from him. He may have had to extend himself to satisfy these expectations and so he developed an anxiety about his ability to indulge his partner. However, once he relaxed his defence mechanisms and realised that everyone has failings, he increased his chance of forming satisfactory relationships.

Usually a permanent relationship was the best way for two people in love to fulfil their needs for each other and that didn't mean that one was using the other, except in mutual interest. An early marriage was recommended for TR because his life might have been influenced for good as his powers of attachment were strong even though he himself might have been a poor marriage prospect due to his unpredictability and his attempts to break away from the conventional.

Career

Early: TR's destiny lay somewhat in his own hands in that his fortune was affected by his innate self-control, conventional notions, acquisitiveness, pride and his organising power. However, his fate depended more on his general surroundings, circumstances, others and particularly his early environment because then there was less power for him to break away from early training and parental influence. His ability to succeed probably came from his parents who taught him to assert himself within the framework of reasonable discipline and responsibility. They supported him in his struggle to make his own way. This early conditioning may also have taught him that he didn't have to get involved with others, or extend a helping hand, if he didn't want to. With this attitude his road to success both in his career and in his relationships would have been paved with frustration and conflict.

It was important for him to become more self-disciplined in developing his talents to improve his competitive position. Self-development was the key and he could have become a credit to himself by building a sound mind in a sound body. As painful as it was, it was absolutely essential that he got some formal education or his fate would have seemed limited indeed. He should have realised that getting an education was a good start. Fortunately, he valued education as the first essential step towards achievement. He knew he could improve his earning ability by being well-informed, so he was willing to invest in getting an education. Learning came easily to him and he rarely forgot what he had learned. He knew that this was the only way to exploit his creativity wisely. He could have made a valuable contribution to society, and he must have had to accept the responsibility for making his creativity available. A vast world of opportunity opened up when he became aware of this. His desire to exploit his creativity may have been frustrated in the beginning but eventually he would have found the freedom to assert himself, when he had learned how to be fully responsible for his actions. His success in striving for significance depended on how well he accomplished this. Deriving the most benefit from it depended on his willingness to satisfy the needs of others. Practical planning and determined self-will united to produce brilliance in management, in science and in unusual ways. Ideals and imaginative intuitions were kept in bounds and given shape and form to make them useful practically. He had found his career in life and had developed a rather uncompromising direction to his life-effort in which he adapted his allegiances to lines along which he could make his efforts count for the most. Overall his practical nature, comprising his executive, businesslike, firm, steady and hard-working traits, would become useful to the world for positions of prominence and responsibility.

Middle: Because a comfortable life was important to TR, the best way to get what he wanted, and to improve the quality of life for others, was through a career that involved public service. His talent for improving existing social conditions was much needed. All he had to find was a way to make a meaningful contribution to society either through personal or group activities, and he was ready to go behind the scenes if necessary. Having a high regard for education he strove constantly to improve his knowledge. Generally, he was willing to change old habits for better ones, so he was rarely locked into an attitude that might have interfered with his continuing progress. His inner and outer worlds were so sufficiently well-integrated that his ambitions didn't run into any serious conflicts with his temperament. The difference between success and failure was the ability to integrate his feelings and will so that emotional distress didn't interfere with his ability to perform well in his career. His chastity was also a key to his success. Because of these considerations his success would have been easier to achieve and he should have gained it fairly early in life.

On a cautionary note, although constructive in a narrow way, order for TR could well have become dreary planning. The resulting mental loneliness led to fear and apprehension that, in turn, produced a lack of poise that forced brusque speech and curt writing.

182

Late: TR had to learn to make appropriate investments to ensure security in later life. With his abundance of ideas he could have done much to shape his future and with a little foresight his financial security and independence would have been assured. He knew that his future financial security must come from using his own resources effectively and he had to discipline himself to do this because being solvent dispelled his anxieties about the future. Through life he was likely to gain money, property, power and dignity, as well as gain from his partner and/or inherited money and possessions. He did have considerable business ability with good economic management. However, he alternated between being preoccupied with money and considering it a cross to bear. Because of that attitude he may have been on the fringes of poverty.

Health

Appearances: TR was just above average height with little that was pleasing in vocal expression or form of body but quick and active in all his movements. TR possessed good health both from nutrition and digestion but the size of his body increased resulting in stoutness. He may have had an extravagant partner.

Health: Though much may have been achieved, his tendency was to overstrain through overdoing thereby impairing his vitality. He should have avoided acting hastily or on impulse, otherwise he ran the risk of physical exhaustion. He was liable to minor accidents and possibly to moods of depression. There was an indication for a premature death of his father and of an easy, honourable death for himself through constitutional weakness.

Throughout his youth (and later) he suffered badly from bouts of asthma. Astrologically we can account for this by the stressful, square of Mars in Scorpio to the Sun in Aquarius at Epoch. This would have been exacerbated by the effect of the afflicted Sun in Scorpio in the 6th House at Birth as well as by the effect of the minor strain aspects received by

Uranus rising in Gemini, in particular from Mars, at Birth. This situation of Uranus could also account for his liability to bronchitis when young. Notice here, that Taurus is rising at Birth (the sign Taurus is associated with the throat) and that the Moon in Scorpio in the 5th/6th House is opposed by Uranus in Taurus at Epoch. His heart trouble, diagnosed when he was twenty, could have stemmed astrologically, once again, from the stressed situation of the Sun in Aquarius being square to Mars in Scorpio at Epoch as well as by the afflicted Sun at Birth. The effect of the opposition here of the Sun to Pluto could account for his frequent liability to diarrhoea when young.
